KT-131-374

hotels • restaurants • shops • bars

singaporechic

For regular updates on our special offers, register at

www.thechiccollection.com

hotels • restaurants • shops • bars

singaporechic

text adrianna tan • joanna greenfield • brandon lee

thechiccollection

managing editor
francis dorai

editor
yamini vasudevan

assistant editor
josephine pang

designer
lisa damayanti

production manager
sin kam cheong

sales and marketing director
antoine monod

sales and marketing managers
rohana ariffin • new bee yong

editions didier millet pte ltd
121 telok ayer street, #03-01
singapore 068590
telephone : +65.6324 9260
facsimile : +65.6324 9261
email   : edm@edmbooks.com.sg
website   : www.edmbooks.com

first published 2006 • second edition 2009
©2006, 2009 editions didier millet pte ltd

Printed in Singapore.

All rights reserved. No part of this publication may be reproduced, stored in a retrieval system, or transmitted in any form or by any means, electronic, electrostatic, magnetic tape, mechanical, photocopying, recording or otherwise, without prior written permission from the publisher.

isbn: 978-981-4217-86-6

1		5			11	13	14	19
2	4				12			20
		7					16	17	
8		10	15			18	21

cover captions:
1: *Enjoy French food in style at Cassis.*
2: *The Halia Aperitif will start a dinner date off on the right foot.*
3: *Shophouses all over Singapore share a distinct architectural style.*
4: *The Singapore Flyer in the evening.*
5: *'Kancheng'—a pot with intricate patterns commonly used in Peranakan households.*
6: *Aerial view of the Formula One circuit.*
7: *A traditional Cantonese dish.*
8: *Couples can enjoy a romantic dinner at Cassis under softly lit arches.*
9: *Jim Thompson offers an array of home furnishings including cushions.*
10: *Halia is the perfect place for some refreshment after a stroll in lush gardens.*
11: *Chinese lanterns are often red in colour, as this is considered an auspicious shade.*
12: *Durian puffs from Goodwood Park Hotel are said to be some of the best available.*
13: *Mint tea served in delicate glasses.*
14: *The Esplanade—Theatres on the Bay— Singapore's premier arts venue.*
15: *Le Bar Rouge is an intimate corner in the trendy supperclub.*
16: *Bangles and other accessories can be purchased from the shops in Little India.*
17: *A dainty handbag from Jim Thompson.*
18: *Shophouse Suites are a trademark of InterContinental Singapore.*
19: *A private room at Peach Garden.*
20: *The chefs at Cassis can do wondrous things with fresh seafood.*
21: *All rooms at Swissôtel The Stamford boast stunning views of the Civic District.*

THIS PAGE: *Flowers are arranged with great care at the Raffles Hotel Singapore.*

OPPOSITE: *Lie back and relax in supperclub with the drinks the waitstaff bring.*

PAGE 2: *The thorns of the Esplanade—Theatres on the Bay when lit up at night.*

PAGE 8 AND 9: *Coloured windows are a unique feature of the MICA building at Hill Street.*

contents

singapore**by**constituencies

Pulau Ubin

Pulau Tekong
Kechil

Pulau Tekong

MALAYSIA

MPINES

EAST COAST

Strait of Singapore

N

Legend

⊕ Airport
○ Lake or reservoir
〰 River
⬤ Above 120 m
⬤ 80–120 m
⬤ 60–80 m
⬤ 40–60 m
⬤ 20–40 m
⬤ 0–20 m

0 km   2.5   5   7.5 km

introduction

modern city-state with a traditional soul

Singapore's skyline is pictorial evidence of a blend of modernity and tradition. The skyscrapers of the financial district—symbols of the city's bustling economy—rise elegantly alongside lush, manicured greens and blend seamlessly with the older shophouses and temples that call to mind life in the early days.

As Singapore is located along the major trade route between the West and the East, maritime trade was, and continues to be, the mainstay of the nation's economy. This in turn laid the foundation for the country's cultural diversity. The flurry of trade brought a mixed group of immigrants, especially Chinese, Indians, Arabs and Europeans. Many used Singapore as a transit point, but some stayed on. Those who made their home here built a nation centred around a multiracial heritage.

Another factor that contributed to the formation of the city's multicultural society was the British administration's decision to divide the island into 'ethnic quarters'. Once the homes of different communities, areas such as Chinatown, Arab Street and Little India have retained the cultural traits of the peoples who inhabited them. As Singapore progressed and advanced to first-world status, every effort was made to sustain its cultural underpinnings. Far from becoming areas of historical interest alone, these places add rich layers of tradition, language and heritage to the Singapore experience.

a global hub

Often described as a 'tiny red dot' on the world map, Singapore has come a long way in the last four decades. In 1965, the country took a giant leap towards complete independence. Many doubted that the move would be a beneficial one. All the odds were against Singapore—it was unfathomable that a city-state with almost no natural resources to speak of, and a total land area of less than 700 sq km (270 sq miles), could sustain itself. However, with self-confidence and foresight, not only did Singapore overcome its limitations of size and lack of resources, it has become one of the most developed and cosmopolitan cities in the world.

The Singapore story is a tale of, among other things, making every opportunity count. The country has demonstrated remarkable resilience in applying determination and integrity into transforming existing strengths, such as the strategic location of its ports, into core competencies. Even irremediable deficiencies, such as the lack of natural resources, could not stand in the way of Singapore's success. Over the years, the city-state has earned its reputation in many fields—as a popular tourist destination, a financial and technological centre, and a much sought-after hub of world-class facilities for arts and sports.

THIS PAGE (FROM TOP): Singapore's ports never sleep—the cranes continue working even through the night; tantalising martinis and cocktails are on offer at any of Singapore's classy bars.

OPPOSITE: A bird's eye view of the Central Business District when the lights come on.

recent and upcoming events

Singapore has played host to many international events, including arts festivals and business summits. In recent years, the country has also carved a niche for itself in sports history as well by hosting a range of tournaments and tours—the most notable achievement being Singapore's ability to lay claim to the fame of hosting the Formula One Grand Prix.

The eagerly anticipated Singapore Grand Prix kicked off on 26 September 2008, and the three nights of exciting races were testimony to the high levels of tenacity and innovation that the world has come to expect of the city-state. Not content to host a regular Grand Prix race, Singapore constructed an impressive street circuit in the heart of the Central Business District, and treated the global audience to the first-ever night race in Formula One history. The spotlights illuminated the Esplanade–Theatres on the Bay, the Old Supreme Court, modern skyscrapers, hotels and the structure of the still-under-construction mega casino-resort at Marina Bay. The event was a huge success, and many are placing bets that the Singapore circuit will be the Asian counterpart to the Monaco Grand Prix.

Unwilling to rest on its laurels, Singapore has been pushing ahead to stage many more such events. The island country was selected as the first Southeast Asian stopover for the Volvo Ocean Race, the prestigious yachting competition. Following 12 months of extensive evaluation, it was confirmed that Singapore would stage the second in-port race of the series in early 2009. In 2008, Singapore was also selected as the venue for the 2010 Summer Youth Olympics.

looking ahead

Looking ahead, Singapore's star is set to shine even more brightly. When the mega resorts at Marina Bay and Sentosa are completed, they will bring with them a bevy of world-class residences, hotels, restaurants and the eagerly anticipated casino—the first in the country. The upcoming range of options for entertainment and leisure have been designed to complement prominent existing establishments, and as well, enhance opportunities for tourism and business. Singapore's success stems from its commitment to remain at the forefront of competition—in business, sports, the arts and entertainment—and this has made it a vibrant destination for those seeking the good life complemented by a luxurious lifestyle.

THIS PAGE: Singapore was the first-ever Southeast Asian stopover for the prestigious Volvo Ocean Race.

OPPOSITE: Renault's Fernando Alonso zooms past the Old Supreme Court, shaking off a year-long drought to achieve a spectacular win. Singapore treated the global audience to a fabulous night race—the first in Formula One history.

PAGE 16: Until today, Singapore is a hotbed of maritime trade.

...Singapore's star is set to shine even more brightly.

architecture

Singapore's buildings tell the story of the country's changing landscape over the years, and the influence of the various elements of history, politics and society. The range of religious institutions and traditional and modern architecture is evidence of the mosaic of cultures that form the core of this nation.

shophouses

Shophouses have always been an integral part of Singapore's cityscape. First built during British rule in response to the arrival of immigrants, the buildings derive their name from their ability to serve two purposes. The double-storey structures were designed so that the lower floor served as commercial space while the upper floor was for accomodation.

The revival of shophouses as chic business spaces have made them sought-after venues for quaint boutiques and offices. Perched on land overlooking Orchard Road, the Peranakan-style shophouses at **Emerald Hill** are among the most stunning examples of this form of architecture. Beautifully conserved and renovated, they are now the premises of several atmospheric bars and restaurants.

temples + churches + mosques

Most of the Chinese migrants came from southern China, and as a result, their temples were constructed in the southern Chinese style. Particularly prevalent are Hokkien or Teochew structures. While much of the materials used were of the highest quality, the builders also devised innovative ways of using recycled materials in their construction—for example, some tiles and rooftop decorations were crafted from parts of ships. Craftsmen reputed for their mastery of the sophisticated art of temple-building were brought specially from China for this purpose. Their skill is evident in the intricate wood carvings expertly etched onto doors, beams and tablets. Prominent examples include the **Thian Hock Keng** (158 Telok Ayer Street) and **Hong San See** temples (31 Mohammed Sultan Road).

The **Chicago Graduate School of Business** (207 Clemenceau Avenue) occupies the House of Tan Yeok Nee, the surviving private mansion of a wealthy businessman. The structure exhibits the balance of yin and yang, while the carvings on the main door relate the story of the Teochews in China's Chaozhou province.

Within the Indian community, architectural differences between the northern and southern regions of India are nuanced but significant. The earliest immigrants arrived from Tamil Nadu in south India, and predictably, their temples were based on the Dravidian style that is common in their home state.

Elaborate spires and ornate carvings are best seen at the **Sri Mariamman Temple** (244 South Bridge Road), **Sri Krishna Temple** (152 Waterloo Street) and **Sri Srinivasa Perumal Temple** (397 Serangoon Road). Visit the **Shree Lakshmi Narayan Temple** (5 Chander Road) to get a glimpse of the variation in structure and style of worship in a north Indian temple.

THIS PAGE (FROM TOP): The elegant minarets of the Sultan Mosque are a trademark feature of Arab Street's landscape; the gopuram or temple spire is a distinctive element of south Indian temple architecture.
OPPOSITE: Shophouses, an integral part of the Singapore cityscape, are now in demand as premises for offices, boutiques and restaurants.

architecture

THIS PAGE (ANTICLOCKWISE FROM TOP LEFT):
The classical dome of Old Parliament House; Corinthian columns characterise the Old Supreme Court building; the tower and spires of the St Andrew's Cathedral make it an important architectural landmark.

OPPOSITE: *The former General Post Office of Singapore, now The Fullerton Hotel Singapore, is a massive waterfront colonial structure with a long history.*

The **Armenian Church** (60 Hill Street) was the spiritual home to the Armenian and Orthodox Christians. Its elegant spire, symmetrical design and Neoclassical style make it one of the most beautiful landmarks of Singapore.

Features such as spires, stained-glass windows and motifs make **St Andrew's Cathedral** (11 St Andrew's Road) and **CHIJMES** (30 Victoria Street) a testament to the illustrious past of local Christian architecture.

Muslim immigrants who came from the Arabian Peninsula, Malay Archipelago, India and Pakistan brought with them distinct architectural styles. The **Sultan Mosque** (3 Muscat Street), located in the centre of the traditional Muslim heartland in Arab Street, has been the focal point for the Muslim community ever since it was built. With its trademark golden dome and Indo-Gothic architecture, the building cuts an imposing figure admist the low-rise shophouses.

The south Indian Muslims built some elegant mosques, such as the **Abdul Gafoor Mosque** (41 Dunlop Street) and the **Malabar Mosque** (471 Victoria Street)—both serene and stunning with their minarets, arches and pastel colours.

The **Dawoodi Bohra Mosque** (39 Hill Street) is an excellent visual example of the different strains of culture within the community. This beautiful mosque, built by the ancestors of the Dawoodi Bohra Shia people, reflects a style that originated in Yemen and South Asia, where the community hails from.

colonial buildings

The British administration left behind several architectural classics that have been preserved with care. Prominent examples include the **Old Parliament House** (1 Old Parliament Lane), the **Old Supreme Court** (1 St Andrew's Road) and the **The Fullerton Hotel Singapore**, which occupies the premises of the former General Post Office (1 Fullerton Square).

modern architecture

Taking a ride on the Singapore Flyer, the giant observation wheel, is probably the best way to appreciate the Singapore skyline—a mix of imposing colonial-era buildings and modern architecture.

No other contemporary structure is as famous as the **Esplanade–Theatres on the Bay** (1 Esplanade Drive), one of Singapore's best-loved sights. Occupying a prominent waterfront location in the Civic District, the Esplanade Theatres' twin aluminum shells are textured with fins that protect the glass façade from the island's hot weather. The fins are also its most distinctive and attractive feature. Since its completion, Singapore's premier arts venue has become an integral part of the skyline, so much so that it's hard to remember what the waterfront looked like before 2002. Looking ahead, all eyes are set to welcome the upcoming **Marina Bay Sands**, featuring three hotel towers topped off by a sky-park and floating crystal pavilions, set among other attractions. The resort will add yet another distinct structure to the range of architectural landmarks that make up Singapore's skyline.

celebrations + festivals

Visit at any time of the year and find yourself surrounded by the swirl and colour of Singapore's ethnic and cosmopolitan fests—evidence of the modern city successfully straddling globalisation and heritage. The multicultural nature of the society makes it one of the few places in the world where festivals with radically different meanings, associations and origins come together cohesively.

ethnic celebrations

The most well-known festivals include **Chinese New Year**, **Deepavali**, **Hari Raya** and **Christmas**. Although they hold special significance for the Chinese, Hindus, Muslims and Christians respectively, all of Singapore participates in the joy of the festivities. About a month before the festivals begin, the respective ethnic neighbourhoods are decorated with lights and ornaments. Tented bazaars spring up to herald the start of the celebrations—vendors sell everything from food to clothes, plants and other items needed for the celebrations. The light-up and shimmering decorations along Orchard Road have become synonymous with Christmas here.

Lesser-known festivals also have a strong following here. An Indian festival that is not widely celebrated elsewhere in the world, even in India, **Thaipusam** is enthusiastically observed in Singapore. Devotees carry milkpots and elaborate structures called *kavadis*, and take part in a procession from Little India to Tank Road. Many of them also pierce spears, needles and skewers into their bodies as a form of penance.

Make sure you visit Chinese Garden during the **Mid-Autumn Festival** to admire dozens of beautiful, delicate lanterns on display. Indulge in mooncakes, a seasonal delicacy that was traditionally made with lotus-seed paste, but is now prepared with a variety of ingredients to satisfy all palates.

Ethnic and religious festivals may be the most celebrated, but in recent years, Singaporeans have also taken to celebrating Western events such as **Halloween** and **Oktoberfest** with much enthusiasm.

food + shopping

The twin national pastimes of shopping and eating are given their own annual festivals—the **Great Singapore Sale**, **World Gourmet Summit** and **Singapore Food Festival**.

The **Singapore Food Festival** celebrates the country's love affair with food with three weeks of culinary workshops, competitions, special deals, and of course, feasting on the best of local and international cuisines.

The **World Gourmet Summit** is a global gathering of top chefs, restauranteurs, sommeliers and others in the industry, during which a select number of Singapore restaurants host Michelin-starred chefs. In recent years the culinary world's superstars like Santi Santamaria and Pierre Hermé have dazzled diners with their special menus and other events. Hotels in Singapore occasionally host their own food festivals and one of the most well-known is the York Hotel's **Penang Hawker Festival**. During most school holidays, the hotel brings in hawkers from Penang to cook favourites like *char kway teow*, flat noodles fried with dark soya sauce.

The **Great Singapore Sale**, or GSS, is a major tourist event that draws thousands from the region and beyond to Singapore. This is one time when shopping, be it for business or pleasure, is taken very seriously—malls throw open their doors until midnight to ensure that little can come in the way of shoppers indulging in retail therapy.

music + the arts

Singaporeans' love for music is exemplified by strong support for events like **Baybeats**, **Mosaic**, **SingFest** and **WOMAD**, which stage top acts in various musical genres to raving audiences. **Mosaic** typically draws the best names in rock, indie and electronic music—Broken Social Scene, Fujiya & Miyagi, the Kings of Convenience, and Sondre Lerche have been past performers; **SingFest** on the other hand is the closest Singapore gets to an outdoor popular music concert, drawing fans of pop artistes such as Jason Mraz, Travis, Alicia Keys and the Pussycat Dolls.

The **SIFAS Festival of Indian Classical Music and Dance** celebrates Indian classical arts of the diaspora. With deep ties to the different schools of the performing arts in India, the performances by local talent and Indian masters alike are always striking and emotive.

Music apart, Singapore has also established its name as an arts centre. The **Singapore Theatre Festival**, **Singapore Film Festival**,

Singapore Arts Festival and the **Singapore Biennale** are major arts events that bring to Singapore the very best that theatre, film and art offer at arts venues such as the Esplanade–Theatres on the Bay, the National Museum of Singapore and The Substation.

The **Singapore Theatre Festival** is a biennial showcase of evocative plays. It is a time when local playwrights, along with established writers from the region, join forces with acclaimed theatre names in Singapore and beyond to present three weeks of memorable plays.

With its finger on the pulse of cutting-edge film from Asia and around the world, the **Singapore Film Festival** screens more than 300 films from 45 countries, and is one of the longest-running film festivals in the region.

THIS PAGE (CLOCKWISE FROM TOP LEFT): Nicole Scherzinger of the Pussycat Dolls performs at Singfest; a model poses in a diamond-studded dress at the launch of the Great Singapore Sale; a film-lover browses the film posters put up during the Singapore International Film Festival.

OPPOSITE (FROM TOP): Colourful lanterns are popular decorative pieces during the Deepavali festival; mooncakes, murukku (a fried snack) and ketupat (rice cakes) are ethnic delicacies served during festivals.

food culture

Singapore's culinary culture operates at impressive levels, with a wide range of local and international cuisines. For those looking to better understand the region's blend of cultures, ethnic and fusion cuisines specific to this part of the world provide the best introduction.

local flavours

It is often said that the best food in Asia is found at alfresco street joints. In Singapore, gourmands and food aficionados can enjoy the best of local dishes served up at food courts and hawker centres.

Famous names include the tourist-friendly **Makansutra Gluttons Bay** (1 Esplanade Drive), **Newton Food Centre** (500 Clemenceau Avenue North) and **Lau Pa Sat** (18 Raffles Quay). Exceptional standouts well known to seasoned food lovers can be found at **Old Airport Road Hawker Food Centre** (Block 51 Old Airport Road), **Golden Mile Food Centre** (505 Beach Road), **Maxwell Road Food Centre** (corner of South Bridge Road and Maxwell Road), **Amoy Street Food Centre** (7 Maxwell Road), **Chinatown Complex** (335 Smith Street), **Ghim Moh** (20 Ghim Moh Road) and **Tiong Bahru Market and Hawker Centre** (30 Seng Poh Road).

Expect to be spoilt for choice at these food centres where there are several rows of stalls and a wide range of food items to choose from. It is hawker centres like these that Singaporeans go to get the best in favourites like *laksa* (noodles in thick curry), chicken rice, fishball noodles and *roti prata* (crisp pancakes). Pick a good stall—one with a good reputation and a long queue—and tuck into any of these dishes. The dining experience at a Chinese *zichar* or stirfry shop, pepper-crab outlets, or tucking into a hearty *sup tulang* (mutton bone soup) is quintessentially Singaporean. Another unusual tradition is eating with your fingers in a typical south Indian restaurant. (Take note though—custom dictates that only the right hand can be used to eat.)

regional tastes

When it comes to restaurants, there are plenty of options, given that Singaporeans love to patronise establishments that live up to their high expectations. Regional Asian and international cuisines are well represented, with a good mix of Italian and French restaurants alongside Chinese, Thai, Japanese, Indian and Nepali eateries.

Regional cuisines are best represented by establishments that cater to Asians living away from their home towns. For those in search of authentic Thai cuisine, **Diandin Leluk Thai Restaurant** and **Nong Khai Beer House** (both at Golden Mile Complex, 5001 Beach Road) serve up Thai dishes as good as any in Bangkok. Another credible option is **First Thai** (23 Purvis Street). Filipino restaurants such as **Kabayan Filipino Restaurant** (Lucky PLaza, 304 Orchard Road) are there for the picking when a craving for *adobo* or *sinigang* strikes.

The best in Japanese fare is available at **Nanbantei** (Far East Plaza, 14 Scotts Road), which is known for its *sake* and *yakitori*, the latter cooked on an authentic grill from Tokyo.

Family-oriented restaurants include **Crystal Jade Dining Place** (IMM Building, 2 Jurong East Street 21), **Imperial Treasure** (Great World City, 1 Kim Seng Promenade) and **Zhou's Kitchen** (Anchorpoint, 368 Alexandra Road). All three establishments are known for their winning formula of refined Chinese cuisine and ambience.

If it is authentic Indonesian or Dutch-Indonesian *rijsttafel* you crave, restaurants like **The RiceTable** (International Building, 360 Orchard Road) and **Pagi Sore** (Far East Square, 88–90 Telok Ayer Street) are sure to hit the spot.

wine + dine

Established restaurants like **Tatsuya** (Park Hotel, 270 Orchard Road), **Aoki Restaurant** (Shaw Centre, 1 Scotts Road), **Iggy's** (The Regent Hotel, 1 Cuscaden Road), **Les Amis** (Shaw Centre, 1 Scotts Road), and **Rang Mahal** (Pan Pacific Hotel, 7 Raffles Boulevard) are among the best in Asia with innovative food, fine wine and impeccable service. Look out also for bistros and restaurants by local talent. These include **Sage, The Restaurant** (7 Mohammed Sultan Road), helmed by Jusman So.

When the Marina Bay Sands and Resorts World Sentosa resorts are ready, they will bring an influx of new restaurants and culinary talent. Stars like Gordon Ramsay, Tetsuya and Nobu have raised the possibility of setting up restaurants in Singapore, testimony that the city-state ranks among top global destinations like Hong Kong and Tokyo in offering the best in food culture.

THIS PAGE (CLOCKWISE FROM TOP LEFT): Fragrant glutinous rice dumplings are available during the Dragon Boat Festival or Duanwu Festival; Raffles Grill serves fine French fare; there is no shortage of delectable dishes involving fresh seafood here; laksa, noodles immersed in thick curry, is a regional specialty.

OPPOSITE (CLOCKWISE FROM TOP): Hawker centres such as Amoy Street Food Centre are a must-visit on a curious travelling foodie's to-do list; fusion fare has gained popularity with Singapore foodies; satay, skewers of meat served with peanut sauce, is a local favourite.

museums + galleries

museums

A showpiece of architecture and history, the **Singapore Art Museum** (71 Bras Brasah Road) is in itself a work of art. Occupying the premises of the former St Joseph's Institution, the museum is well known for its art exhibitions and sculptures.

The multidisciplinary exhibitions, displays, lectures, festivals and workshops at the **National Museum of Singapore** (93 Stamford Road) make it one of the foremost cultural destinations in the country. The **Asian Civilisations Museum** (1 Empress Place) houses 11 galleries with over 1,300 artefacts—part of the museum's growing collection from the civilisations of China, Southeast Asia, South Asia and West Asia.

Sculpture Square (155 Middle Road) is an independent gallery of sculpture and contemporary 3D art from Singapore and the region.

For a glimpse into the histories of the ethnic communities in Singapore, drop by the **Chinatown Heritage Centre** (48 Pagoda Street), **Eurasian Heritage Centre** (139 Ceylon Road) and **Malay Heritage Centre** (85 Sultan Gate). The **Peranakan Museum** (39 Armenian Street) provides a look into the culture of the Straits Chinese community, with entire rooms used to replicate real-life settings.

Independent museums and galleries cover the whole gamut from art to design and toys. More than 50,000 toys dating from the mid-19th century can be found at the **MINT Museum of Toys** (26 Seah Street), including vintage collectibles and Chinese comic book covers.

The **Children Little Museum** (40 Kandahar Street) celebrates the 1950s and the 1960s with its displays of the various scenes typical of the era, as well as a collection of toys, school books, passports and even mobile cinemas of the day.

The Japanese Occupation during the Second World War deeply affected the lives of many Asians and Allied prisoners of war—Singapore was no different. **The Changi Museum** (1000 Upper Changi Road North) and the **Reflections at Bukit Chandu** (31 K Pepys Road) honour the memories of those bleak years with stories and exhibits of tragedy and triumph.

art + galleries

Singapore's art scene is nascent, but one that is constantly growing. The old guard of Singapore artists—illustrious names such as Chua Ek Kay, Tan Swie Han, Chen Wen Hsi and Lim Tze Peng—have added much to the genres of Chinese and Western ink and oil paintings here, while emerging young talents like Brian Gothong Tan, Heman Chong and Tan Ling Nah are drawing international attention with their work in multimedia, installation and sculpture, which are part of the upcoming developments in the art scene in Singapore.

Venues that display contemporary art include **Art Forum** (82 Cairnhill Road), **Art-2** (MICA Building, 140 Hill Street), **Eagle Eye Art Gallery** (Stamford House, 39 Stamford Road), **Art Focus Gallery** (176 Orchard Road) and **Studio 83** (83 Kim Yam Road). In addition, contemporary and experimental art spaces at **Emily Hill**

(11 Upper Wilkie Road), **Plastique Kinetic Worms** (61 Kerbau Road) and **Post-Museum** (107 and 109 Rowell Road) provide thought-provoking, alternative perspectives.

Singapore is also a great venue for viewing art from around the region—artists from India, Indonesia, Vietnam, China, and even Laos are well-represented at the galleries that dot the city. These include **Bodhi Art Gallery** (11 Unity Street, Robertson Walk), **Gajah Gallery** (MICA Building, 140 Hill Street), **Linda Gallery** (Block 15, Dempsey Road), **M Gallery** (1 Kaki Bukit Road) and the **Luxe Art Museum** (6 Handy Road).

Galleries are not the only places to browse for outstanding art pieces. The private art collection of the **St Regis Singapore** (29 Tanglin road) easily ranks among the finest in Asia, with Fernando Botero sculptures, Joan Miró sketches and paintings by contemporary Asian artists as well.

The Ritz-Carlton, Millenia Singapore (7 Raffles Avenue) houses an astonishing 4,200-piece modern art collection, including masterpieces by renowned artists Frank Stella, Andy Warhol and Dale Chihuly. The hotel's breathtaking architecture itself is the work of Pritzker Prize-winner Kevin Roche.

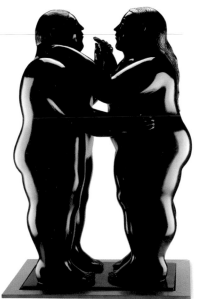

THIS PAGE (CLOCKWISE FROM TOP LEFT): The Peranakan Museum houses items from Straits Chinese families; the St Regis Singapore boasts an impressive art collection; explore the food gallery at the National Museum of Singapore. OPPOSITE: Interior of the National Museum of Singapore.

nature

Given that Singapore's total land area is less than 700 sq km (270 sq miles), it may seem that there is not much land for botanics. Yet, Singapore possesses a number of pristine spots, some with complex ecosystems.

green trails + parks

Singapore's proximity to the equator may have contributed to the island's lush landscape. However, the country's efforts to maintain its reputation as a garden city also played a key part. Singaporeans are surrounded by nature, from tree-lined streets to gardens and well-maintained parks.

Favourite scenic destinations include **MacRitchie Reservoir** (off Lornie Road) and **Bukit Timah Nature Reserve** (177 Hindhede Drive). The award-winning **Singapore Botanic Gardens** (Cluny Road) has something for everybody, including activities like music concerts if you are looking for more than just a walk in a park.

The new **HortPark** (33 Hyderabad Road), which cost $13 million to build, is a premier nature and lifestyle hub with 20 themed gardens, a treetop walk and restaurants. The HortPark also features diverse pods of nature within, such as the Silver Garden, Golden Garden, Fantasy Garden, and Herb and Spice Garden. The park also connects **Telok Blangah Hill Park** (near Telok Blangah Green) and **Kent Ridge Park** (off South Buona Vista Road), two quiet and pristine spots.

Not far from the bustle of downtown Singapore, the **Fort Canning Park** (Fort Canning Centre) is one of the most historical spots in Singapore. Once termed the

Forbidden Hill, the park still houses Sir Stamford Raffles's house, and was also used as a military base during the Second World War.

The **Fort Canning Spice Trail** houses nearly 100 types of herbs and spices, and features information regarding their varied qualities, as well as culinary and medicinal uses.

farms

Singapore may be importing most of its food, but organic farms have been cropping up in parts of the island.

At **Bollywood Veggies** (100 Neo Tiew Road), visitors can check out vegetable farms and dairies, buy organic vegetables, as well as explore pottery workshops and art galleries, before settling in for lunch at the Poison Ivy Bistro.

Join Ruqxana of **Cookery Magic** (179 Haig Road) as she takes her students on a farm tour. After picking the required vegetables, she conducts her famous cooking class on-site.

Similar classes are also run in **Pulau Ubin** (boat ride from Changi Jetty) a rustic village and nature haven, a short boat ride away from northeastern Singapore. Still densely forested, the island is popular among cycling, trekking and camping enthusiasts.

Pulau Ubin is also home to the remarkable **Chek Jawa**, probably Singapore's most renowned spot for marine life. With a number of rare ecosystems thriving within a small area, Chek Jawa is regarded by nature-lovers as the best place to look out for marine life, especially rare species such as horseshoe crabs and peacock anemones.

THIS PAGE (CLOCKWISE FROM TOP LEFT): Many of the island's parks boast water features teeming with life; health buffs thoroughly enjoy jogs around the Telok Blangah Park; Pulau Ubin is a hotspot for watersports, with competitions being held here on a regular basis.

OPPOSITE: The lush greenery of the Singapore Botanic Gardens makes it one of the most popular outdoor spots in the country.

the high life

Given Singapore's reputation as a playground for the rich and famous, options abound if you have a love for luxury. Travel to neighbouring regions in style or pick up a special timepiece that will serve as a treasured memento of the good times.

travel

Singapore's strategic location affords plenty of opportunity for regional travel, with the lure of nearby exotic destinations too strong to resist. The pristine beaches of Malaysia, Thailand, Cambodia and Indonesia are never too far away.

An even more tempting option can be found close at hand. Merely 85 km (53 miles) away, near the Indonesian island of Bintan, is the private island of **Nikoi**—available for booking in its entirety, with six exclusive villas and a breathtaking view of the South China Sea.

Few luxury experiences can surpass the notions of grandeur and romance that train travel conjures up, particularly the images of luxe cabins, butlers and meals aboard moving restaurants with sparkling silverware. For the full experience, take a trip aboard the majestic **Eastern & Oriental Express** (reservations to be made via email at oereservations.singapore@orient-express.com), better known as the **E & O**. The service between Singapore and Bangkok departs from the train station at Tanjong Pagar, and travels to Bangkok through the countryside, villages and rice fields of Malaysia and southern Thailand. The journey into the heart of Asia—in sublime luxury—is unparalleled.

The E & O also offers a cruise service to Burma, called the 'Road to Mandalay'. Get a glimpse of a world that seems to have been untouched by time, and marvel at nature's beauty as the cruise liner gently glides along the Ayeyarwaddy River.

Sail your own way to preferred destinations by chartering a yacht from the **il Lido** (Sentosa Golf Club) restaurant on Sentosa Island. Excellent Italian dishes will be served on-board your beautifully outfitted boat.

If you prefer to fly, book a private jet from **Taj Air** (Thong Sia Building, 30 Bideford Road) to get to the heart of India, the city of Mumbai.

timepieces

High-flyers have always had a strong love for fine timepieces, but rather than buying just any watch off the rack, pick up an exclusive piece from **Vacheron Constantin** (Ngee Ann City), carried only by select retailers.

Singapore's importance as an international centre for the watch trade means that international watchmakers have as much of a significant presence here as local and regional horologists demand.

While getting a bespoke watch made is possible, the time taken to custom-make a piece may be regarded by some as too long.

A delightful alternative is offered by the watch retailer **Sincere Haute Horlogerie** (Hilton Gallery), which works with top watchmakers around the world to create a special selection of watches that are only available in Singapore, and only in limited numbers.

THIS PAGE (ANTICLOCKWISE FROM TOP RIGHT): Pick up an exclusive timepiece from the world's best watchmakers; charter your own luxury yacht and set sail on a romantic cruise; silverware and table service complete the idyllic setting aboard the Eastern & Oriental Express.

OPPOSITE: The Eastern & Oriental Express chugs its way through scenic vistas on the journey from Singapore to Bangkok.

theatre + music

The creative industry in Singapore may not seem large in comparison with that of some other countries, and it wasn't too long ago that theatre-, music- and film-lovers could be heard expressing their hopes for more support for the arts scene. Yet, despite the nation's relatively small size and population, there are several theatre outfits and the quality of creative output is significant, and headed for the better.

theatre

Theatre in Singapore is a lively enterprise involving the English, Mandarin, Malay and Tamil languages. Major theatre productions are presented throughout the year by Singapore companies such as **W!LD RICE**, **The Necessary Stage**, **Singapore Repertory Theatre** and **TheatreWorks**. Other companies also have busy theatre schedules, such as Mandarin group **Drama Box**, Malay companies

Teater Ekamantra and **Teater Artistik**, Tamil group **Agni Kootthu** and bilingual company **Toy Factory.**

A common trend has been the tendency on the part of the playwrights to use the stage as a medium to voice their opinions on cultural norms. Playwrights such as Alfian Sa'at, Ng Yi-Sheng, Haresh Kumar and Elangovan have also used the stage as the setting to stimulate dialogue on controversial issues.

Alongside local talent, major international theatre groups such as the **Royal Shakespeare Company**, the **SITI Company** and **Mabou Mines** have performed in Singapore during art festivals and tours.

In addition, well-known groups from Asia and Southeast Asia that are at the forefront of theatre, such as the **Ming Hwa Yuan Taiwanese Opera Company,** have also made Singapore a regular pit stop.

music

Singapore's music scene was in its infancy until recently. Music critics might share the opinion that Singapore's music industry has lingered perilously within the domain of the safe and boring for far too long. With commercial viability in mind, local talents have tended to follow regional or international trends, with an emphasis on English and Mandarin pop.

However, prominent music labels have turned this trend around, and begun to bring home-grown talents to the fore. Established local musicians like **Electrico**, **The Observatory** and **Corrinne May** have blazed the trail for other Singaporean singer-songwriters by achieving a degree of local and international success.

Emerging young bands like **The Great Spy Experiment** and **B-Quartet** are also following suit. Given that Singapore has attracted some of the best-known names during events such as WOMAD or SingFest, there seems to be no lack of inspiration for local talents.

Jazz musicians have enjoyed success in the region and beyond. They are led by talented siblings **Jeremy** and **Clarissa Monteiro**, who have enjoyed remarkable careers.

Local music can be found at several venues around the city. The best bets are **Timbre** (The Substation, 45 Armenian Street), **Prince of Wales** (101 Dunlop Street), **Bar None** (Marriott Hotel, 320 Orchard Road), **JAZZ@SOUTHBRIDGE** (82b Boat Quay) and **Home Club** (The Riverwalk, 20 Upper Circular Road).

THIS PAGE (ANTICLOCKWISE FROM TOP RIGHT): Ian Watkins performing at Singfest; Tamil theatre group Agni Kootthu during a performance of '1915'; Singapore boasts local talent such as the Wicked Aura Batucada, a contemporary percussion group.
OPPOSITE: The Necessary Stage puts up several performances every year.
PAGE 34: A view of the city's impressive skyline with its newest addition, the Singapore Flyer.

orchardroad

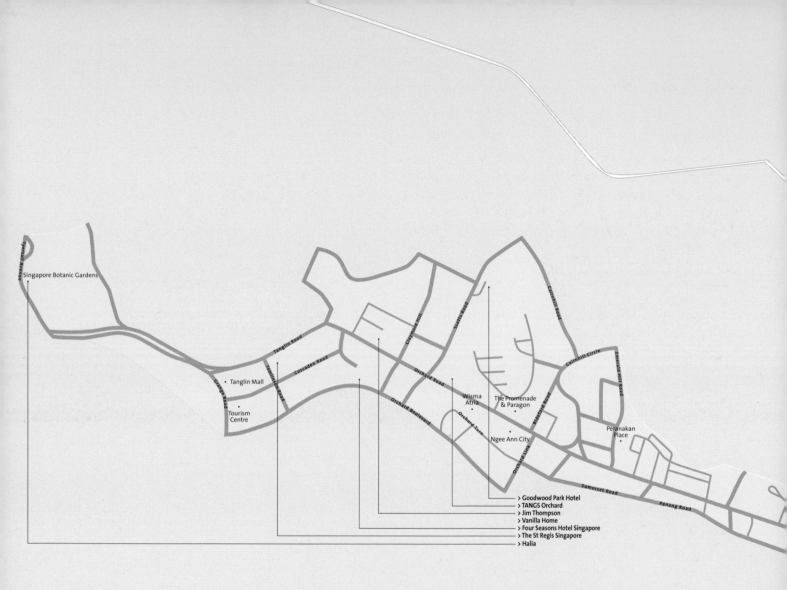

Tyersall Avenue

Singapore Botanic Gardens

Tanglin Road

Cluny Road

Grange Road

Tanglin Mall

Tomlinson Road

Cuscaden Road

Tourism
Centre

Orchard Boulevard

Paterson Hill

Orchard Road

Scotts Road

Cairnhill Road

Wisma
Atria

The Promenade
& Paragon

Orchard Turn

Bideford Road

Cairnhill Circle

Emerald Hill Road

Peranakan
Place

Ngee Ann City

Orchard Link

Somerset Road

Penang Road

> Goodwood Park Hotel
> TANGS Orchard
> Jim Thompson
> Vanilla Home
> Four Seasons Hotel Singapore
> The St Regis Singapore
> Halia

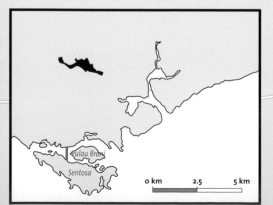

Pulau Brani

Sentosa

0 km   2.5   5 km

Legend

Main Ro
Other Ro

0 m   100   200   300

orchard road

The tree-lined avenues of Orchard Road and its environs once threaded through pepper plantations and fruit orchards, after which the area is named. These days the trees line one of Asia's premier shopping belts with its endless malls and the perennial stream of human traffic.

Despite a growing number of new malls in other parts of Singapore, Orchard Road's popularity as a shopping haven has never been challenged. Contrary to expectations that upcoming shopping stretches elsewhere might overshadow Orchard Road, new shops, bars, and even entire malls consistently crop up in this area, bringing together luxury names in shopping and dining from around the world.

the best in retail therapy

Orchard Road's star quality is the abundance of choice for any and every indulgence, whether it's in high fashion, jewellery, art, beauty products, street wear, watches or home furnishing. Touted as having the highest concentration of shopping malls in Asia, Orchard Road is also home to the flagship boutiques of many major-league brands.

If the likes of Manolo Blahnik, Jil Sander and Stella McCartney are your preferences, look no further. Serious fashionistas will appreciate the convenience of proximity—with luxe brands concentrated within the compact stretch of central Orchard Road, power shopping is as easy as flitting from one boutique to the next.

In addition, home-grown and regional Asian brands compete to tempt the discerning shopper, especially those looking for special finds. A couple of malls even have sections dedicated to fine cuisine for those who might wish to pick up gourmet cheese or wine.

best times to visit

The annual Great Singapore Sale is probably the most awaited event of the year for Orchard Road's patrons. Residents apart, visitors often plan their trip around it to ensure they don't miss this event. Throughout the sale, fashion trends are unveiled and the season's best picks are up for grabs. Malls keep their doors open late into the night, and little can come in the way of a full day of shopping.

Come Christmas, Orchard Road boasts some of the most lavish decorations—massive ornaments adorn the entrances of major shopping centres and thousands of lights illuminate the streets. To get a glimpse of the best in Christmas festivities, you need look no further.

THIS PAGE: Spoilt for choice, a shopper contemplates her next stop inside the deluxe shopping mall, Paragon.

PAGE 36: From morning til late in the evening, Orchard Road and its surroundings are a buzzing hive of activity.

THIS PAGE (FROM TOP): Unwind with a glass of champagne after an intense retail therapy session; branded shoes, clothing, accessories, homeware— whatever you need, the shops in the district will deliver.

OPPOSITE: This life-sized poster is an illustration of Orchard Road's reputation as chic shopping destination.

more than just shopping

While a quick stroll along Orchard Road might leave some with the impression that it has little more to offer beyond retail indulgence, nothing can be further from the truth. There are several little oases of peace, many of which are tucked away from the hustle and bustle of the main stretch of malls, ideal for weary shoppers looking to rest their feet.

Small boutique cafés and bars dot the landscape, each offering a variety of drinks and finger food—perfect places to sit back and read a book, watch the crowds or plan the rest of the day. Walk up to the charming restaurants and bars in the former Peranakan enclave of Emerald Hill, where carefully restored Straits Chinese-style shophouses form the backdrop for a special evening. Keep a lookout as well for special offers from major hotels in the area for lazy Sunday brunches with endless good food and champagne, and high teas with select local delicacies.

The cosmopolitan character of Orchard Road's establishments is evident in its sampling of ethnic cafés and restaurants, which cater to expatriates craving a taste of home. Especially suited for the culinarily adventurous, they offer an opportunity to discover new cuisines and flavours from around the region—definitely well worth the break from your shopping spree.

Just minutes away from Orchard Road, the Singapore Botanic Gardens' 52 hectares (130 acres) of greenery includes, lakes and even a tropical rainforest. The Botanic Gardens also house some of the city's best-known dining establishments.

everything for everyone

For those visiting Singapore, a trip to Orchard Road is usually the first item on the agenda. Often seen as a shopping haven, Orchard Road is better described as a hub where different lifestyles come together. Fashion divas pick and choose from the collection of Asian and international designer labels; watch-lovers can take their time choosing the best of Swiss timepieces to invest in; street-wear lovers flock to the limited edited sneaker stores and street-label collectives; and antique shops beckon those who wish to pick up special mementoes. This kaleidoscope of options represents the best of Singapore's shopping scene, making Orchard Road the irresistible destination that it is—and there are plans to make it even better.

Set for an expected $1.6-billion rejuvenation, Orchard Road and its surrounding areas will soon feature landscape and infrastructural enhancements. Aside from new shopping venues that will significantly increase the diversity of retail options, the main street will feature Urban Green Rooms. These will serve as shady resting places and as areas for exhibitions and mini-performances, with special lighting to enhance the botanics at night. In addition, street parades and outdoor fringe activities during special events promise to liven up a visit to this area.

...a hub where different lifestyles come together.

restaurants + bars + cafés

While some may associate high-end dining with style over substance, Orchard Road's stalwarts have kept the bar high on both counts.

dining: asian + international cuisines

If award-winning Chinese cuisine is what you're after, there are classic Cantonese dishes refined to perfection at **Hua Ting** (Orchard Hotel) and innovative contemporary cooking at **Jiang Nan Chun** (Four Seasons Hotel Singapore).

Din Tai Fung (Paragon), which originated in Taipei, brings its famous *xiaolongbao* dumplings, steamed chicken soup and beef noodles to its Singapore outpost. Other places that offer favourites like *dim sum* include the **Crystal Jade Palace** and **Imperial Treasure Nan Bei** (both at Ngee Ann City). The much-loved **Kam Boat Chinese Cuisine** (Shaw Centre, 1 Scotts Road) offers roast meats and a superlative crab roe porridge—a mix of creamy porridge and a generous serving of crustacean roe, a seasonal rarity.

Iggy's (The Regent Singapore), a modern European restaurant regarded by many as an institution, has won several accolades, including the honour of being the only Southeast Asian restaurant to be included among the World's 100 Best Restaurants.

Housed in a black-and-white bungalow, **The Song of India** (33 Scotts Road) is where Milind Sovani works to create Indian culinary wonders. The Song of India offers traditional cuisine spiced up with modern cooking techniques.

THIS PAGE (CLOCKWISE FROM TOP LEFT): An assortment of sweets and desserts wraps up a meal of fine Indian fare at The Song of India; at Iggy's, dainty culinary creations such as this will thrill one's palate; savour fantastic cuisine from the kitchens of Iggy's in the restaurant's carefully appointed dining room.
OPPOSITE: A sparkling chandelier drapes down from the ceiling of The Indigo Mist, one of the private dining rooms in The Song of India.

Top-notch Japanese restaurants **Aoki** (Shaw Centre) and **Tatsuya** (Park Hotel Orchard) are best known for their highly rated *omakase* and lunch sets. **Tenshin** (The Regent Singapore) specialises in *tempura*, while **Nanbantei** (Far East Plaza) is the *kushiyaki*-lover's default option, with authentic charcoal-grilled skewers.

Join Japanese food aficionados at **Kazu Sumiyaki** (Cuppage Plaza) for a taste of the delectable *yakitori*. Sample a hearty *ramen*, simmered for eight hours and served with pieces of roast pork along with a runny stewed egg at the **Noodle House Ken** (Orchard Plaza). This is accompanied by ample Asahi and Kirin beer.

Step into **Shashlik** (Far East Shopping Centre) for a trip back to the past. The bright lights of Orchard Road give way to retro furnishing and dim lighting—the perfect setting in which to savour old-school *shashlik*, *borsch* and baked alaska.

The adventurous should venture into **Kabayan** (Lucky Plaza) to sample *adobo*, *sinagang* and other specialties from the Philippines. **Ayam Bakar Ojolali** (Lucky Plaza), which means 'unforgettable grilled chicken' in native Javanese, serves up chicken dishes worthy of its name, as well as impressive barbecued fish.

The Les Amis group established its reputation as one of the best in fine dining with its first outlet, **Les Amis** (1 Scotts Road). The group-owned **The Canteen** (Shaw Centre) redefines Singaporean classics such as crab *mee pok* (made with flat yellow noodles) while sister establishment **La Strada** next door offers excellent Italian courses. Also

restaurants + bars + cafés

THIS PAGE (ANTICLOCKWISE FROM TOP): While away a lazy afternoon at Halia in the Singapore Botanic Gardens; a host of delicacies covering every course of a meal is served at Halia; sweets and pastries are served for tea at The Drawing Room.

OPPOSITE (ANTICLOCKWISE FROM TOP): StraitsKitchen's exhaustive wine list complements its local fare; cocktail-lovers are spoilt for choice, given the range of bars in this area; The Marmalade Pantry's casual gourmet fare is a hit—the Ultimate Beef Burger is a fan-favourite.

part of the group, **Au Jardin Les Amis** (1 Cluny Road) is the perfect marriage of elegance and the natural beauty of the Singapore Botanic Gardens.

Also in the gardens is **Halia** (1 Cluny Road). Named after the Malay word for 'ginger' this alfresco restaurant is much-loved for its wonderful food and scenic setting.

Grand Hyatt Singapore's (10 Scotts Road) acclaimed restaurants, **mezza9** and **StraitsKitchen**, are among the finest dining options in the city. mezza9's open-kitchen concept features nine varied dining experiences, while StraitsKitchen is a celebration of Singaporean delights.

The Shangri-La Hotel Singapore's (22 Orange Grove Road) **The Line** offers an opulent buffet spread around the clock, with a focus on fresh seafood and tempting desserts.

relax and unwind: cafés + bars + clubs

After a long day, rest your feet at **Hediard** (123-125 Tanglin Road) or at the **Royal Copenhagen Tea Lounge** (Takashimaya Department Store). Hediard's luxury breakfast and brunch sets feature *foie gras*, caviar and salmon; while the the Royal Copenhagen Tea Lounge's delectable high tea is always a treat.

For tea lovers, **The Rose Veranda**'s (Shangri-La Hotel Singapore) high tea with 101 different types of tea on offer is a must-try. Afternoon tea at **The Drawing Room** (St Regis Singapore) is an experience not to be missed—tasty canapés and pâtisserie are served on elegant china, to be enjoyed with tea or coffee.

The Marmalade Pantry (Palais Renaissance) has built up a loyal following for its gourmet burgers, sandwiches and desserts, while the PS Café (Paragon) boasts time-tested favourites like *laksa* pesto pasta and banana mango crumble. Canelé Pâtisserie Chocolaterie (Shaw Centre) serves a range of organic teas and savoury crêpes, but it is aptly famed for its artisanal cakes and different varieties of macarons that tempt the sweet-toothed.

To experience a traditional Singaporean café, head down to Killiney Kopitiam (67 Killiney Road). Sample *kaya* (coconut jam) toast and *kopi* at their best, and take home a jar of freshly-made *kaya*. Or pick up breads and cakes that live up to their name from Freshly Baked by Les Bijoux (57 Killiney Road), run by a former pastry chef from the Saint Pierre restaurant.

No 5 Emerald Hill Cocktail Bar (5 Emerald Hill), set in a charming shophouse, is one of the best in the area. Sister pubs Ice Cold Beer (9 Emerald Hill) and Que Pasa (7 Emerald Hill) are set apart by the extensive beer list in the first outlet, and the wine menu in the second.

The Grand Hyatt Singapore's award-winning mezza9's martini bar has over 30 cocktails listed on its menu, with well-known favourites such as the chrysanthemum-tinged 'Sakura martini'.

Over the years, Marriott Hotel Singapore's (320 Orchard Road) Bar None and Living Room have been Orchard Road's leading bars—with fantastic music and classy settings, it's not hard to see why.

shopping

Every shopper's dream, Orchard Road is a treasure trove for retail indulgence. The stretch from **Four Seasons Hotel Singapore** (190 Orchard Boulevard) and **Hilton Singapore** (581 Orchard Road), to **Ngee Ann City** (391 Orchard Road) and **Paragon** (290 Orchard Road) offers the best in all things luxurious.

clothes + shoes + accessories

Power shopping is the order of the day in Orchard Road, with **Club21** for men and women (Four Seasons Hotel Singapore) leading the charge. With top brands like Marc Jacobs, Alexander McQueen, Martin Margiela, John Galliano and Dries Van Noten, Club21 is the first stop for cutting-edge fine fashion. The folks behind Club21 also run the **iSHOP** (Orchard Cineleisure, 8 Grange Road), selling Macs, iPods and related accessories.

On a smaller scale, **The Link Boutique** (Meritus Mandarin Hotel) has a carefully curated selection of latest trends and enduring classics— brands like Stella McCartney and cult-celebrity favourite, Pocket Venus. Look out for alldressedup, a Singaporean label that has won many accolades for its principal desinger Sven Tan's fresh take on contemporary style. **Eclecticism** (Wisma Atria) stocks bags, jewellery and clothes from almost 30 independent labels like Sobella, Orla Kiely, 575 Denim, Charlotte Ronson and Ella Moss in an endearing little boutique.

Some of the best brands in clothing, shoes and perfume are to be found at the **Hilton Gallery** (Hilton Singapore). Fans of Issey Miyake's

THIS PAGE (FROM TOP): Mumbai Se brings the best in high-end Indian fashion to this part of the world; for the best of luxury shoes and bags, Orchard Road is your stop.

OPPOSITE (CLOCKWISE FROM LEFT): Lingerie models strut down the catwalk showcasing Triumph's collection at the Singapore Fashion Festival; items from Shanghai Tang's line of bold outfits and stylish accessories are a must-have for fashionistas; the perfect piece of silverware awaits you at Evnur Solid Silver.

PAGE 48: Decanter at The St Regis Singapore features more than 1,500 labels of exquisite wine.

clothes and fragrances will love the flagship **Issey Miyake** store, a veritable temple to his innovative couture, while **Mulberry**'s country-chic line of bags will be joined by an anticipated range of women's shoes designed by Jonathan Kelsey. More top brands such as **Balenciaga**, **Jil Sander**, **Marni** and **Louis Vuitton** also have their flagship stores here.

Shoe-lovers should turn their heads and heels towards the first Southeast Asian flagship **Manolo Blahnik** store (Hilton Singapore), or

saunter over to **On Pedder** (Ngee Ann City) for designer footwear, handbags and accessories by Jimmy Choo, Junya Watanabe and Christian Louboutin. **The bagbar** (Paragon) puts a novel spin on designer-bag retail by showing off beautiful bags from Chloé, Judith Leiber and the like in the lush interiors of a bar.

Fans of high-fashion street-wear will be right at home at **Surrender** (119 Devonshire Road), co-owned by UNKLE's James Lavelle stocking his Surrender label, in collaboration with

Singaporean street-wear designer Earn Chen. Housed in a leafy suburb off Orchard Road, the store also carries brands like Head Porter, Original Fake and Maharishi.

For a bold taste of ethnic designs from China and India, there are the avant-garde styles by globally known labels **Shanghai Tang** (Ngee Ann City) and **Mumbai Se** (Palais Renaissance, 390 Orchard Road). Both labels cater to stylish trendsetters with pieces that add a touch of ethnic elegance to modern designs.

Walk over to the other side of Orchard Road to **Déjà vu Vintage** (The Cathay, 2 Handy Road), a store that carries only one of each piece of clothing and each accessory, carefully sourced from around the world.

If you are looking to invest in silverware, **Evnur Solid Silver** (Tanglin Mall, 163 Tanglin Road) is a haven of choice. With a range of contemporary or traditional European and Turkish designs, every piece is unique and crafted with minute attention to detail.

four seasons hotel singapore

THIS PAGE: *Newly refurbished, the guestrooms are now even more opulent than before.*

OPPOSITE (FROM LEFT): *Jiang-Nan Chun, on the second floor, serves Cantonese fare which has been prepared to perfection in a stylish and distinctly Chinese setting; the lovely lobby warmly welcomes guests to the hotel.*

Nestled in the exclusive enclave of Orchard Boulevard, Four Seasons Hotel Singapore is only a few steps away from the shopping, entertainment and business belt of Orchard Road, and not far from the tranquil Singapore Botanic Gardens. It is also a convenient 15-minute drive away from the Central Business District and the Marina Bay area—an ideal location that allows for both business and leisure. The contemporary façade of the hotel belies its grand and gracious interiors, which evoke a feeling of timeless elegance. Housed within is a treasure trove of some 1,500 Asian and international artworks.

Each of the 255 rooms, which include 40 suites, is designed for maximum comfort, style and efficient use of space. Freshly refurbished, the Four Seasons Hotel Singapore now offers rooms with interior design by the celebrated Hirsch Bedner Associates.

These redesigned rooms feature elegant textured wall fabrics, and are appointed with furnishings in soothing tones of mocha, beige and ivory. The décor in these rooms exhibits some Asian influence as well, which can be found in the lush carpets patterned with plum blossom motifs, the Chinoiserie-inspired artworks adorning the rooms, and the *objets d'art* and furniture, which reflect a tasteful blend of Asian and European styles.

Technological gadgets and thoughtful amenities are offered in all rooms for the guests' convenience. These include high-speed Internet access, wireless connectivity, international multi-pin electrical sockets, MP3 player docks, VGA ports that allow guests to connect a computer to the 107-cm (42-inch) flat-screen television in each room, CD, DVD and VCD players, individually controlled air-conditioning and a customised Four Seasons bed for the ultimate comfort at bedtime.

Available to all guests, Four Seasons Hotel Singapore's recreational facilities include a fully equipped gym that is open around the clock, two pools and two outdoor tennis courts. In addition, a full service spa offers a comprehensive range of pampering beauty and body treatments.

...grand and gracious interiors, which evoke a feeling of timeless elegance.

rooms
255 rooms, including 40 suites

food
One-Ninety: local and international ·
Jiang-Nan Chun: traditional Cantonese

drink
The Bar and Alfresco

features
collection of Asian and international art ·
2 ballrooms · health club · 2 pools · spa ·
car and limousine hire · 24-hour room service ·
2 air-conditioned indoor tennis courts ·
business centre · 2 outdoor tennis courts ·
full audio-visual support in function rooms ·
wireless connectivity · Category 6 high-speed
Internet access

nearby
Orchard Road · sightseeing · shopping ·
museums · bars and clubs · dining ·
Singapore Botanic Gardens

contact
190 Orchard Boulevard, Singapore 248646 ·
telephone: +65.6734 1110 ·
facsimile: +65.6733 0682 ·
website: www.fourseasons.com/singapore

Enjoy exceptional dining at Four Seasons Hotel Singapore. The contemporary One-Ninety delights visitors with its modern international and local cuisine. Its lavish Sunday Brunch features a selection of over 50 delectable dishes served at interactive food stations, while a dedicated children's play area provides entertainment for younger guests. The hotel's award-winning Jiang-Nan Chun is synonymous with style and classic Cantonese cuisine, and its discreet service makes it the venue of choice for many society dinners, power lunches and casual family reunions. Afternoon tea at The Bar and Alfresco is one of the many pleasurable rituals that every visitor should indulge in after some retail therapy at the adjoining designer arcade and Orchard Road's collection of shopping centres.

With 14 straight years of international and local awards and accolades under its belt, the hotel has firmly established a reputation for superlative service and reaffirmed its position as the venue of choice for discerning business travellers as well as guests on vacation.

goodwood park hotel

Singapore does not suffer from a lack of grand colonial hotels. However, one that keeps a foot in its past and another firmly in the modern age is Goodwood Park Hotel. It was originally constructed as the Teutonia Club in 1900 for the German expatriate community.

Having survived two world wars—pretty much unscathed—the hotel's tower is now gazetted as a national monument. With so much history it would be easy for Goodwood Park Hotel to get wrapped up in the style of the past, but it has taken the far more challenging path of constant renovation. While grand dames run the risk of appearing dated, the hotel presents a timeless classic style in a much simpler way—one that is undoubtedly more sophisticated. With a beige, cream, grey and peach colour palette, the effect is understated yet warm, and details are kept to a minimum to avoid clutter.

Rooms vary in size, and all are decorated with contemporary finishes. The suites each have a private sitting room, while some boast a second bedroom for family members or last-

THIS PAGE (FROM TOP): The hotel's distinctive façade extends visitors a warm welcome; the Rose Marie Suite's spacious lounge is ideal for entertaining friends.

OPPOSITE (CLOCKWISE FROM TOP LEFT): The Coffee Lounge presents patrons with a new look but retains the same flair for local dishes that it has always had; if Orchard Road is too far away, Min Jiang @ One-North is certainly a viable option for some fine Chinese cuisine; the hotel has gained a reputation for producing some of the best-tasting durian puffs available on the island.

rooms

110 Deluxe rooms • 8 Deluxe Poolside rooms •
15 Tower Rooms • 14 Junior Suites •
3 Deluxe Suites (one- or two-bedroom) •
13 Poolside Suites • 5 Deluxe Poolside Suites •
Rose Marie Suite • 64 Parklane Suites

food

Coffee Lounge: local specialities and high tea •
Gordon Grill: Continental •
Deli: cakes, pastries and cookies •
Min Jiang and Min Jiang @ One-North: Chinese •
L'Espresso: lunch, dinner and English high tea

drink

Highland Bar • L'Espresso

features

fitness centre • 2 pools • 2 ballrooms • spa •
weddings • same-day laundry service •
business centre • boardroom • concierge •
24-hour room service

nearby

Orchard Road • Newton • Ngee Ann City •
American Club • Far East Plaza • TANGS •
Shaw Centre • Wheelock Place • Wisma Atria •
Singapore Botanic Gardens

contact

22 Scotts Road, Singapore 228221 •
telephone: +65.6737 7411 •
facsimile: +65.6732 8558 •
email: enquiries@goodwoodparkhotel.com •
website: www.goodwoodparkhotel.com

minute additions to the party. Others open out onto Goodwood Park Hotel's manicured gardens and two pools.

But the hotel's crowning jewel is the stunning Rose Marie Suite, once described as one of the most beautiful suites east of the Suez. Its spacious lounge, leather-panelled study, luxurious bedroom with a walk-in closet, bathroom installed with a sauna and grand dining room, accompanied by its own roof-top garden, certainly justify the accolade. Served by a private lift, it just doesn't get any better or more exclusive.

Dining at Goodwood Park Hotel is always an experience. Local events and festivals inspire food fairs throughout the year, and visiting chefs spice up the programme on a regular basis. Perhaps the most notable of the hotel's several restaurants is the Coffee Lounge. In existence since the 1970s, the Coffee Lounge has been through a dramatic revamp. Now, its stylish symmetrical décor is complemented by a grid-like fixture hanging from the ceiling. For food, the restaurant remains a reliable choice for local specialities, as it has been since its opening.

Craving something Western? Gordon Grill is renowned for its steak and the famous meat trolley. Meanwhile, Min Jiang offers specialities from Szechuan and other parts of China—nowhere else in Singapore can one enjoy authentic Peking duck and *dim sum*. Due to its growing popularity, Min Jiang has branched out and moved into a black-and-white colonial house in Rochester Park.

In all, the Goodwood Park Hotel wins visitors over with its modern style and its endearing link with the past. What's more, although the hotel is conveniently sited—Orchard Road is literally five minutes away—its location on the top of a hill ensures that the hordes of snap-happy tourists are kept away. No one will drop by to disturb you while you are having breakfast.

the st regis singapore

When staying at the St Regis Singapore, guests bask in the lap of luxury as soon they step off the plane. With a room reservation comes the option of booking a transfer in one of the hotel's customised Bentleys, as well as access to Changi Airport's highly exclusive JetQuay terminal. After such an extraordinary start, the VVIP welcome continues upon arrival at the hotel, where the staff is at the ready to open doors and move guests' belongings inside. Already aware of every guest's name and particulars, the check-in process is seamless.

Designed by the highly acclaimed Wilson Associates, the hotel interior and guestrooms are stately and stylish. Each room comes complete with original artwork, designer fabrics and customised chandeliers. As with everywhere else in the hotel, the attention to detail is what makes the guestrooms so special—from heated bathroom mirrors that don't steam up to comfortable beds with 15 types of pillow; from a BOSE sound system connection for guests' iPods to an unpacking and packing service courtesy of the St Regis Butler. There are no coffee or tea-making facilities in the rooms, but rest assured, the butler will prepare each guest's beverage of choice—a bedtime hot chocolate for the little one, or a latte or cappuccino for that early morning wake up call.

THIS PAGE: All guestrooms are appointed tastefully and are well-equipped to provide the utmost in comfort and luxury—the Executive Deluxe room is a fine example of this.

OPPOSITE (FROM TOP): Brasserie Les Saveurs serves tasty French and international dishes in a bright, cheery setting; pull up to the lobby in style in one of the hotel's Bentleys.

Making its debut in Asia is one of the hotel's key features, the Remède Spa. Guests will be introduced to it straight off the bat, as Laboratoire Remède provides the room amenities stocked in each guestroom.

Setting the spa apart is its diversion from spa clichés. Gone is the new-age music and in comes the jazz, Baroque, Bosa Nova or other genres patrons may fancy. Gone is the squeaky-clean menu of spa cuisine and juice; champagne and chocolates are recognised as beneficial for the body too. Without the usual earthy Asian feel, Remède focuses on water in all its healing forms. Indeed, bathing is the highlight here; on-site, there is a marble Vichy shower room where the signature Black Olive Eucalyptus Soap Scrub is performed, a hammam, cedarwood saunas, ice fountains and both indoor and outdoor hydromassage whirlpools, among other amenities. The use of the spa facilities is all part of the hotel service, and guests can immerse themselves in the best in spa therapy in beautifully appointed treatment rooms if they so wish.

The attention to detail continues into the St Regis Singapore's restaurants and bars. Decanter holds wine tastings every day from 5.30 pm for an hour with the sommelier. Astor Bar reinvents the signature Bloody Mary from its flagship hotel, the St Regis New York. In Singapore, this favourite cocktail becomes the Chilli Padi Mary, made with chilli, old ginger and lemongrass—sheer genius! The hotel's Mediterranean restaurant, LaBrezza,

serves cuisine ranging from Lebanese and French to Italian and Middle Eastern. Brasserie Les Saveurs offers international and French fare in a fine dining setting, and Yan Ting has a superb set lunch menu and great *dim sum*.

It's increasingly obvious how special this hotel is; in 2008 alone, the St Regis Singapore was included in well-known publications such as *Condé Nast Traveler*, in its 'Hot List', and *Travel + Leisure*, in its annual 'It List', among others. The hotel has one of the finest private art collections in Asia, including pieces by Fernando Botero, Frank Gehry and national treasure Chen Wen Hsi, an air-conditioned tennis court with amazingly high ceilings and the best location on upper Orchard Road.

rooms
299

food
Brasserie Les Saveurs: French and international • The Drawing Room: tea and snacks • LaBrezza: Mediterranean • Yan Ting: Cantonese

drink
Decanter: wine • Astor Bar: cocktails

features
Bentley fleet • airport transfers • concierge • air-conditioned indoor tennis court • spa • fitness centre • butler service • 24-hour business centre • 8 meeting rooms • John Jacob Ballroom • secretarial services • broadband wireless Internet

contact
29 Tanglin Road, Singapore 247911 • telephone: +65.6506 6888 • facsimile: +65 6506 6788 • email: stregis.singapore@stregis.com • website: www.stregis.com

halia

A walk around the Singapore Botanic Gardens always appears on the Singapore must-do list, regardless of the length of one's stay. The superb landscaping, Orchid Garden and numerous coffee shops and cafés make it an obvious tourist spot, but it is the various fine-dining establishments that make the Botanic Gardens a worthwhile visit for everyone.

One of these noteworthy restaurants is Halia. Ensconced in the Ginger Garden, Halia (Malay for 'ginger') was named after its lush—and surprisingly colourful—setting. Very much a part of the landscape, Halia was built as the garden was being developed. As a result, it fits seamlessly with its surroundings rather than spoiling it. Hidden among the greenery, it is a job to find, but that is all part of its charm. Halia by night is a romantic affair, lit by discreet lamps and candles. By day, the full-

length windows provide an excellent view of the lush foliage surrounding the restaurant. Tables out on the deck allow guests to sit directly in the midst of the greenery. Even better, live jazz performances during dinner every second and last Sunday of the month help soothe any Sunday night blues.

Halia serves brunch on weekends and public holidays. Afternoon tea from Mondays through Saturdays provides yet another opportunity to take in the verdant surroundings in a leisurely manner. On Sunday mornings, Halia offers traditional breakfast items, such as freshly made muesli with fruit and honey, alongside a more gourmet selection. Some examples of the latter include truffle-scented egg white scramble with sturgeon caviar and *foie gras torchon pâté* on brioche, accompanied by a glass of champagne. For afternoon tea,

THIS PAGE (FROM TOP): Nestled in the Ginger Garden, Halia offers a unique dining experience; the food served here includes a tantalising array of meat and seafood dishes.

OPPOSITE (FROM TOP): Villa Halia is the restaurant's newly added extension, and is a great place for private or corporate events; similar to many of the beverages on the menu, the Halia Aperitif contains ginger.

seats
Halia: 40 indoors, 70 outdoors •
Villa Halia: 60 in Wine Bar, 50 in Courtyard,
50 in Gallery Room

food
Continental with Asian influence

drink
Wine Bar • signature ginger-based cocktails
and mocktails

features
facilities for private functions and corporate
events • local art • live jazz • catering •
garden setting

nearby
Orchard Road • Tanglin Mall • Ginger Garden •
Dempsey Village • National Orchid Garden •
Singapore Botanic Gardens

contact
1 Cluny Road (enter via Tyersall Avenue)
Ginger Garden, Singapore Botanic Gardens,
Singapore 259569 •
telephone: +65.6476 6711 •
facsimile: +65.6476 4502 •
email: info@halia.com.sg •
website: www.halia.com.sg

Halia may well be the only restaurant in Singapore that serves fresh scones with ginger-infused cream and ginger jam.

For lunch and dinner, the cuisine is predominantly European, but peppered with Asian nuances. Ginger is an example of these predominant Asian flavours, and it is used in varying degrees throughout the menu: the Shrimp Satay Salad comes with a pomelo-and-ginger flower dressing, and for dessert, the Teh Tarik Halia—a caramel tea *crème brulée*—is served with a refreshing ginger sorbet.

Even the drinks menu is spiced up. Served in a pair of test tubes, the pre-dinner Halia Aperitif contains vodka, cherry brandy, fresh ginger and sparkling Prosecco. The Halia Infusion, which can be served both hot and cold, is another perfect accompaniment to dinner. Special mocktails and cocktails are also available—the signature Ginger Jive, which has ginger juice blended with honey, fruit punch and orange juice, is a great choice.

A new addition is Villa Halia; here local artists display their work in the wine bar and gallery. The tapas menu ensures a more relaxed feel and the three distinct areas—the Wine Bar, Gallery Room and Courtyard—are ideal for private functions. Dedicated fans may be pleased to know that Halia has just opened its first overseas outlet, Halia Hanoi. Soon the Halia experience will be available in more places around the world!

jim thompson

Convinced that Thai silk could capture the imagination and interest of buyers all around the world, James Thompson—better known as Jim Thompson—established the Thai Silk Company after World War II. He and his company are widely credited for reviving Thailand's dying silk industry and bringing its many products to the attention of the world.

In 1967, Jim Thompson disappeared under mysterious circumstances in Cameron Highlands, Malaysia. By then however, the industry had grown by leaps and bounds. Today, the company he founded is still going strong—its success may even have exceeded his expectations. Supplying shoppers with a wide range of products, the company also has an established presence throughout Asia and around the world.

Here in Singapore, there are five Jim Thompson outlets scattered about the island. All of these stores offer an impressive array of Thai silk products, from home furnishings and decorative pieces to clothing and other fashion items and gifts.

For the home, the stores carry ornaments such as silk cushions. The latter are available plain, printed or textured, all in vibrant colours meant to add brightness and warmth to the home. Coordinated place mat and napkin sets can also be purchased here.

THIS PAGE (FROM TOP): Although the company has expanded in other directions, it will always be most famous for its fabrics; home furnishings are available for purchase in the Jim Thompson stores.

OPPOSITE (FROM TOP): Ladies may wish to spend some time browsing through the handbags and beach bags; the company's fabrics are used in the production of a huge variety of goods.

The company has also branched out into furniture, producing distinctive, East-meets-West collections that highlight contemporary Thai design. Ed Tuttle, Ou Baholyodhin and Christian Duc are some of the designers involved in this endeavour, and they have produced several collections. Pieces include daybeds, armchairs, sofas, occasional tables and bedside tables, each crafted from solid timbers and exquisite fabrics. Among the varied selection of gift items and accessories available for purchase at the many Jim Thompson stores are purses, picture frames, cigarette and spectacle cases, wine sacks, tissue holders, vanity kits and jewellery boxes.

For children, collectors or the young-at-heart, there are adorable teddy bears and stuffed toy elephants made from silk, cotton and chenille. The emphasis of course is on the lustrous fabrics that are most evident in the variety of fashion items on offer.

Women can choose from a ready-to-wear collection of plain or printed silk blouses, skirts and scarves, while for men there are shirts and neckties. Regardless of whether formal or informal, plain or flamboyant, all of Jim Thompson's products merge unique Thai elements with contemporary designs.

Of course, customers can also purchase plain or printed silk and cotton fabrics for clothing as well as for upholstery; fabric is the company's speciality, after all. Jim Thompson carries several fabric collections which encompass a whole range of designs and colours, all of them equally lovely. The Angkor Collection, In Wonderland Collection, The Voyager Collection, Ottomania Collection and The Muses Collection are only a few examples of the wide array that is on offer.

Jim Thompson has also diversified into dining establishments such as restaurants, bars and cafés, primarily located in Malaysia and Thailand. The first outlet of this type to make an appearance in Singapore is a restaurant by the name of Jim Thompson on Dempsey, which opened its doors to hungry guests at the end of 2008. Serving lunch, dinner and brunch—although this last is only available on Sundays—the restaurant will surely bring to the table the same high quality that has made Jim Thompson a household name in Asia.

products
Thai silk · clothing · gifts and accessories · home furnishings

features
contemporary Thai furniture

nearby
shopping · dining · sightseeing · city tours · cinemas

contact
Palais Renaissance: 390 Orchard Road, #01-08 & #02-10, Singapore 238871 ·

Takashimaya: 391 Orchard Road, Ngee Ann City B1, Singapore 238873 ·

DFS Scottswalk Level 1: 25 Scotts Road, Singapore 228220 ·

Raffles Hotel Arcade: 1 Beach Road #01-07, Singapore 189673 ·

telephone: +65.6323 4800 ·
email: siamsilk@singnet.com.sg

tangs orchard

THIS PAGE: TANGS is a one-stop shopping venue, stocked with everything from household goods to fashion accessories.

OPPOSITE (FROM TOP): The first floor offers patrons an array of branded beauty products; after hours of browsing, indulge in some refreshments at the Island Café.

TANGS has been one of the premier shopping destinations in Singapore for almost 80 years, and still remains so today. A prominent player in the vibrant Singapore retail arena, TANGS has always responded well to changing consumer trends. The company continually strives to break new ground and set new benchmarks within the industry; it seeks to achieve these goals through innovative store design, unique merchandising concepts, creative marketing and service excellence.

The flagship store, TANGS Orchard, is housed in an iconic building that boasts green-tiled roofs and red pillars—a distinctive sight on Orchard Road. Even today, it is the place shopaholics head to when they need to purchase everything from exquisite crockery and cutlery to designer clothing.

With a collection of speciality concepts spread over five floors, TANGS caters to the fashion and lifestyle needs of its discerning clientele. The merchandise is sourced from all around the world and placed alongside products from TANGS's own exclusive labels. The goods on offer are categorised by concept and lifestyle, an easy-to-understand method of organisation that helps to provide an enjoyable shopping expedition.

The basement and first floor are occupied by TANGS Home and TANGS Beauty Hall. The former stocks everything one requires in a home, from bed linen to kitchenware, and the latter, beauty products. At TANGS Beauty Hall, shoppers will find designer scents, collectible fragrances from Annick Goutal and L'Artisan Parfumeur, body and bath products from Molton Brown, as well as internationally renowned brands such as Benefit, Kiehl's, La Prairie and Bulgari.

The second floor is ladies' heaven, with Wardrobe Women offering brands such as Martina Pink and STUDIOTANGS. Any woman will be able to select a whole new ensemble, with accessories and shoes to match, from the array of female apparel available on this floor.

Dressing Room on Level 2 is a girl's world of ultimate pampering as she shops for intimate apparel in the plush setting of a boudoir. With its warmly lit themed dressing

products

men's, women's and children's fashion ·
beauty products · fashion accessories · shoes ·
educational toys · electronic gadgets ·
homeware · kitchenware

features

DHL service point · local delivery service ·
frequent launch shows and events ·
TANGS loyalty card · personal shopping ·
Island Café · TANG+Co

nearby

Orchard Road · Singapore Botanic Gardens ·
shopping · dining · sightseeing · city tours ·
cinemas

contact

310–320 Orchard Road, Singapore 238864 ·
telephone: +65.6737 5500 ·
facsimile: +65.6734 4714 ·
email: customer_service@tangs.com.sg ·
website: www.tangs.com

rooms, which boast large, polished mirrors and velvet-covered walls, the Dressing Room offers a unique shopping experience. This sensual setting is perfect for the items on offer here.

Male shoppers are not forgotten. On the third floor, Wardrobe Men carries the exclusive label, LIBRARY, which supplies men with all the fashionable office wear they need, right down to their cufflinks.

Also located on this floor are Technobay—where gadgets such as digital cameras, game stations and timepieces from renowned brands are to be found—and PlayLab. The latter carries global street-wear brands for men and women.

An offshoot of TANGS, TANG+Co offers the modern fashion elite a range of merchandise that promises 'new luxury'. The women's line covers all the bases with over 20 big-name brands from all over the globe such as, Alannah Hill, Stella Forrest, Tara Jarmon and Antik Batik. Also available are shoes, bags and accessories from BCBG Girls, Beverly Feldman, Ras, Luana and more. Ladies will have no trouble finding a complete outfit for every occasion. Similarly, TANG+Co Men offers quality fashion collections from around the globe, with labels such as David Mayer, Armand Basi and John Varvatos.

The shopping experience at TANG+Co is enhanced with plush furnishings, designer lighting, soothing music and exceptional personal service provided by TANG+Co Fashion Associates. Equipped with trend tips and style advice, they discreetly offer their assistance when it is required. All in all, TANGS Orchard is a one-stop shopping venue that will probably still be going strong for another 80 years.

vanilla home

THIS PAGE: *The store is practically an Ali Baba cave, full of treasure to be discovered.*

OPPOSITE (FROM TOP): *The items are arranged so tastefully that it is sometimes difficult to tell which are for sale and which are part of the interior design; Vanilla Home imports its products from the crème de la crème of designer brands in Europe and Argentina.*

In recent years, the once-staid island of Singapore has become something of a cool-hunter's dream, in the way that only the most rapidly developing cities can. At present, traditional businesses exist—only sometimes harmoniously—alongside newer designer establishments, borrowing from one another to create new forms and experiences that many travel here to find.

The most prescient of creative developers saw this coming, of course, and one of the first to realise the potential of this new climate was Stefanie Hauger, an interior architect who opened her first Vanilla Home outlet in a Chinatown shophouse. The venture quickly garnered attention disproportionate to its modest locale, and greatly enriched the Singapore design scene with its ultra-chic collection of lifestyle products that were, prior to that time, unavailable in the region. Her clientele soon expanded to include architects, professional designers and art directors from around the region, all drawn by a kinship with the individual aesthetic of Vanilla Home and its owner.

Utilising her finely tuned judgement and experience in interior design, Hauger created a showroom space of understated refinement to complement the carefully chosen lamps and furnishings on offer. Each item is deservingly treated as an art piece, without exception chosen for its character, quality and visual appeal. Virtually every single item was specially selected from a pool of leading European designers and brands.

The original store's success has resulted in the opening of a new boutique showroom, one that enjoys the company of leading luxury labels in Singapore's dynamic Orchard Road district. Housed on the first floor of the upscale Palais Renaissance shopping centre, the new outlet of Vanilla Home has found an even wider base of appreciative patrons.

products
decorative lamps · furniture · soft furnishings · porcelain · crystalware · artwork

features
imported European and Argentinian designs · wedding list

nearby
Orchard Road · Singapore Botanic Gardens · The Istana · cinema · designer boutiques

contact
390 Orchard Road, #01-07 Palais Renaissance, Singapore 238871 ·
telephone: +65.6838 0230 ·
facsimile: +65.6738 8720 ·
email: contact@vanilla-home.com ·
website: www.vanilla-home.com

With staff that are friendly and yet unobtrusive, the in-store shopping experience has been designed to offer customers the space and time needed to explore the store and contemplate every decision thoroughly— no purchase is too small to warrant careful consideration of its place in the home. Should it be necessary, expert assistance is never far away, with a cup of coffee, a second opinion or a word of recommendation.

Embellishing the walls are the works of a number of talents who are represented by the company, among them: photographer Russell Wong, oil painter Irene Hauger and artist Ketna Patel. Their contributions to the living room atmosphere blend beautifully with the lush lounge soundscape compiled and mixed by the owner herself, creating a cocoon of style and artistic substance.

Some of the items that can be found here include household necessities by Plata Lappas, Buenos Aires; hand-painted Limoges porcelain by Alberto Pinto of Paris; hand-crocheted toys from Annie Claire Petit of The Netherlands; lamps and printed glass and mirror furniture from London's Porta Romana and Knowles & Christou, respectively; exquisite lamps by Emily Todhunter of London; and silk Fortuny lanterns by Venetia Studium, Venice. The lifestyle emporium also carries a range of coffee-table books from Taschen, Thames & Hudson, Flammarion and Rizzoli.

From the beginning, Vanilla Home has been—and indeed, still is now—a godsend to discerning homeowners and collectors everywhere. There are plans to launch a collection of its own in 2009, which will surely make a visit worthwhile.

civicdistrict

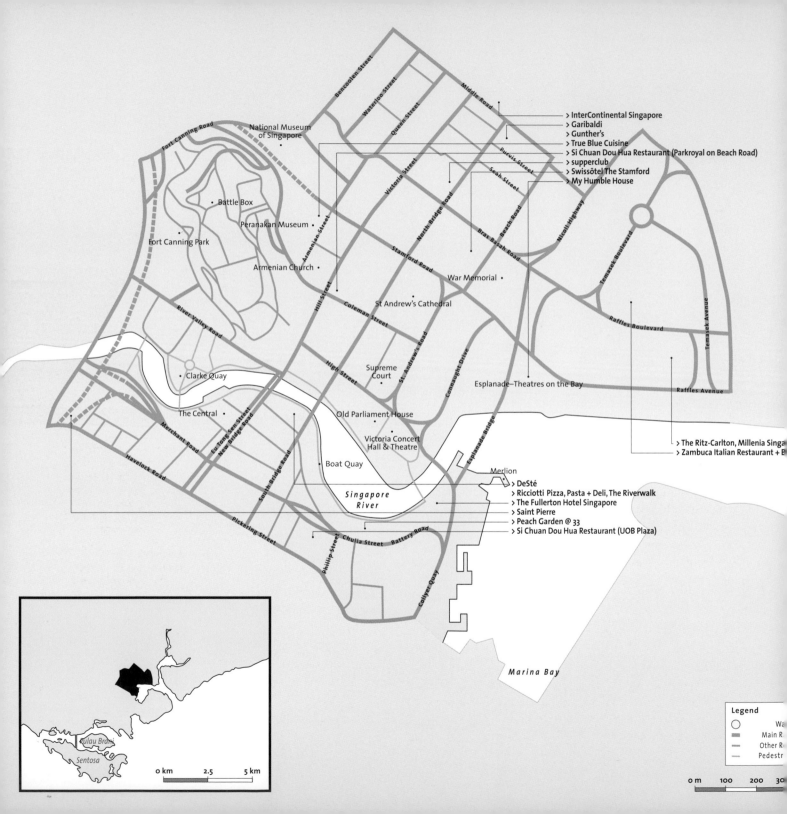

> InterContinental Singapore
> Garibaldi
> Gunther's
> True Blue Cuisine
> Si Chuan Dou Hua Restaurant (Parkroyal on Beach Road)
> supperclub
> Swissôtel The Stamford
> My Humble House

National Museum
of Singapore

Battle Box

Peranakan Museum

Fort Canning Park

Armenian Church

Bencoolen Street
Waterloo Street
Queen Street
Middle Road
Victoria Street
Purvis Street
Seah Street
North Bridge Road
Bras Basah Road
Beach Road
Nicoll Highway

Fort Canning Road
Armenian Street
Hill Street
Stamford Road
Coleman Street

War Memorial

St Andrew's Cathedral

River Valley Road

Clarke Quay

The Central

Merchant Road

Eu Tong Sen Street
New Bridge Road

Havelock Road

Pickering Street

High Street
Supreme
Court
St. Andrew's Road
Connaught Drive

Old Parliament House

Victoria Concert
Hall & Theatre

Boat Quay

South Bridge Road

Phillip Street
Chulia Street
Battery Road

Collyer Quay

*Singapore
River*

Esplanade—Theatres on the Bay

Esplanade Bridge

Raffles Boulevard

Temasek Boulevard

Temasek Avenue

Raffles Avenue

> The Ritz-Carlton, Millenia Singa
> Zambuca Italian Restaurant + B

Merlion

> DeSté
> Ricciotti Pizza, Pasta + Deli, The Riverwalk
> The Fullerton Hotel Singapore
> Saint Pierre
> Peach Garden @ 33
> Si Chuan Dou Hua Restaurant (UOB Plaza)

Marina Bay

Pulau Brani

Sentosa

0 km   2.5   5 km

Legend

◯   Wa
▬▬▬   Main R
▬▬▬   Other R
▬ ▬ ▬   Pedestr

0 m   100   200   30

civic district

When the world turned its eyes on Singapore during the Formula One Grand Prix night race held in September 2008, the spotlight shone brightly on the impressive street circuit in the Civic District. A blend of the old and new formed a glimmering backdrop: the Corinthian columns of the Old Supreme Court, the Padang's expanse of green, the distinctive shimmering fins of the Esplanade–Theatres on the Bay, and the city's skyline gleaming in the distance, punctuated by the hotels and skyscrapers of the financial district.

visual history

Shaped to serve as the centre of administration during British rule, the Civic District houses the country's best in historical architecture. These buildings, once the premises of government offices, courts, recreational clubs and concert halls, stand testimony to the enduring nature of the Civic District as the financial and administrative nerve centre of Singapore.

Classic examples of colonial architecture include the Old Supreme Court and Old Parliament House, both of which were built in the neo-Palladian styles. The Corinthian columns of the Old Supreme Court are specific iconic symbols of the building styles of that period. The grand dame of the Civic District is the majestic National Museum of Singapore, where Modernist extensions fuse effortlessly into the Neoclassical building to form an elegant piece of architecture. The former General Post Office, now The Fullerton Hotel Singapore, is an oft-quoted example of the Palladian style. Another example of colonial-era architecture, and the largest remaining Victorian filigree cast-iron structure in Southeast Asia, is Lau Pa Sat. Once a produce market, the building has been restored, and is now a favoured food centre in the area

Located atop a hill, the Fort Canning Park was the site of military fortifications and governors' residences during British rule. Its key advantage is the bird's eye view of the island. A significant component of Malay legends, the park is believed to be the resting place of the last Malay king. Minutes away from the city, Fort Canning Park has several historical attractions, but it is the the outdoor music concerts held here throughout the year that draw the crowds.

While the influence of the colonial era is exemplified by landmarks such as the Old Supreme Court and National Museum of Singapore, the end of British rule and the years of Japanese Occupation are portrayed by the Civilian War Memorial and The Battle Box.

PAGE 64: The Esplanade Bridge, as seen from below.

THIS PAGE (FROM TOP): Aerial view of the street circuit constructed in and around the Civic Distric for the Formula One Grand Prix race; a close-up view of the metal fins of the Esplanade–Theatres on the Bay, one of its most distinctive features.

business and entertainment enclave

The Central Business District on the periphery of the Civic District is the heart of Singapore's financial and corporate hub. Innumerable skyscrapers dot the landscape—testimony to the growing presence of Singapore as a regional and global business hotspot.

Come nightfall, the surrounding areas of Clarke Quay and Boat Quay cater to the shopping, dining and nightlife needs of the district's executives as well as visitors. The quays were once the sites of busy warehouses, merchant offices and jetties. Their primary purpose was to handle the unloading and storage of goods brought in by ships and boats. The rows of shophouses have since been restored, and now form the premises of posh nightspots, cafés and restaurants. Alfresco dining is a popular option here, with the Civic District's skyline forming a perfect backdrop along the Singapore River.

There are several activities to indulge in apart from dining and shopping. Take a ride on a old-fashioned *trishaw*, or cruise down the waterway in an authentic 'bumboat' to explore the sights of the quays in a different light. Watch the different processes involved in the art of pewter making by going on the Royal Selangor Process Demonstration Tour and creating your very own masterpiece while participating in the Royal Selangor's School of Hard Knocks course.

Those who love an extreme adrenaline rush should try the G-Max Reverse Bungy located at Clarke Quay. Designed and developed in New Zealand eight years ago, the G-Max carries up to three people in a specially designed open-air, steel-reinforced capsule, which is then catapulted up to 60 m (197 ft) in the air at speeds of 200 km (124 miles) per hour.

upcoming landmarks

Work is underway on the Marina Bay Sands resort and casino, which will be centred around three hotel towers topped by a sky-park, retail stores featuring cutting-edge labels, restaurants run by celebrity chefs, chic nightclubs and Singapore's first casino. Business facilities also abound—visitors on business can avail of the meeting halls and a convention centre that can host over 45,000 delegates.

The Civic District is a compact area in a compact city, but the plethora of things to see and activities to indulge in makes it a good place to explore—and given the speed at which it reinvents itself, it appears unlikely that this area will relinquish its reputation as the most exciting part of the city-state anytime soon.

THIS PAGE (FROM TOP): The thrilling G-Max Reverse Bungy will give you the ride of your life, if you dare take up the challenge; the dining and entertainment enclave of Clarke Quay is the choice destination for worn-out executives looking to relax after a long day's work.

OPPOSITE: The heart of the Central Business District—the office buildings of Raffles Place brightly illuminated at dusk.

...the heart of Singapore's financial and corporate hub.

beauty + shopping

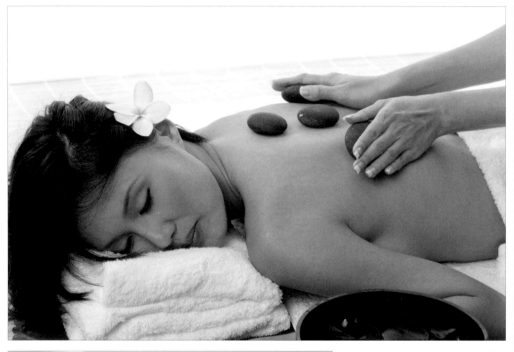

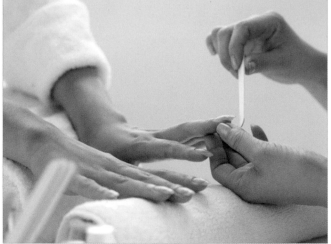

THIS PAGE (FROM TOP): Soothe tired muscles and frazzled nerves with a hot-stone massage; expert manicurists help to keep your nails in perfect shape, and ensure it is done in good time too.

OPPOSITE (ANTICLOCKWISE FROM TOP): Bags on display at a store window tempt shoppers to come in and browse; Jim Thompson is the place to pick up stylish home décor items; executives can purchase smart suits and office-wear from the speciality shops that dot the area.

high-speed beauty

Beauty centres in the Civic District are aware of the high expectations and time constraints of their clientele, and ensure that they do not disappoint. You can be sure you have put yourself in trustworthy hands for the best in grooming.

The nail-care experts are spot on with their manicure and pedicure services at **FE The Nail Lounge** (Raffles City Shopping Centre), while eyebrow architects **Browhaus**'s (Suntec City) full suite of grooming services ensure that furrowed brows are impeccably shaped and trimmed. For a session that combines indulgence with beauty, make an appointment with **PASSAGE New York** (133 Cecil Street).

A renowned name in spa, massage and reflexology, **Kenko Wellness Spa**'s (Esplanade Mall) 10-minute shoulder massage is popular with professionals looking to relax during lunch.

fashion + shopping

Executive fashion does not have to be boxy or boring, as home-grown **Swirl** (Stamford House) demonstrates. Swirl carries homemade designs and a range of other labels, including skirts and dresses from Dotted Line.

For suave shirts and cufflinks that combine classic styling with contemporary flair, shop at the Singapore outlet of British label **Thomas Pink** (Capital Tower, 168 Robinson Road).

Some of the best shopping options are located within the Raffles Hotel Arcade. Admire the products made from pure Thai silk at **Jim Thompson**, or have a shirt custom-made to perfection by the tailors at **CYC–The Custom Shop**. To bring home your purchases in style, pick up exclusive travel bags from **Samsonite Black Label**.

Footwear lovers will adore **Sole 2 Sole** (Millenia Walk, 9 Raffles Boulevard) for its collection of shoes from United Nude and Nicholas Tate.

The best fragrances from Grasse and beyond are to be found at **Senteurs de Provence** (Millenia Walk, 9 Raffles Boulevard), which also offers perfumery workshops.

A good place to look for edgier fashion pieces, **Actually** (29A Seah Street) carries brands like Freitag and Headquarter. Have your pick of fashion and lifestyle products by home-grown designers at **Designed in Singapore** (24 Mohammed Sultan Road).

Art-lovers can shop for prints, sculptures and other accessories at the famed **Metropolitan Museum of Art Store** (Raffles City Shopping Centre). Those who wish to take home music CDs and books as special mementoes can find them at **Earshot Café** (1 Parliament Lane), as well as Singaporean films at **Sinema Old School** (11B Mount Sophia).

The range of furniture and accessories from renowned international brands like G.O.D, Purple Room and Blackbook at **Anthropology** (Raffles City Shopping Centre) makes it the top stop for stylish homeware.

Kokon Tozai Boutique + Café (Singapore Flyer) carries an impressive collection of handmade kimonos, ties and handbags, offering a unique blend of modern appeal with traditional elegance.

restaurants + bars + cafés

restaurants

Top-brass restaurants **Saint Pierre** (3 Magazine Road) and **Le Saint Julien** (The Fullerton Waterboat House) are renowned for their French cuisine and impeccable service. *Yakitori* specialist **Torisho Taka by Aoki** (1 Nanson Road) serves amazing grilled meats, curry rice and *ramen*.

Morton's (Mandarin Oriental Hotel) famed grain-fed beef is available in generous portions of steak or in complimentary steak sandwiches with every martini order at their popular Mortini Nights.

The InterContinental Singapore offers a wide range of wine and dine options, including the **Olive Tree Restaurant** and **KŌ**. For a private, exclusive dinner, reserve your place at **Chef Chan's Restaurant** (National Museum of Singapore)—a restaurant with only seven tables set amidst the chef's collection of Chinese antiques.

For the best in neo-classic Chinese cuisine, look no further than **My Humble House** (Esplanade Mall). A member of the Tung Lok Group, My Humble House's chefs fuse aesthetic appeal with gastronomic excellence in all their creations.

For casual lunches, try the sandwiches and burgers at **Epicurious** (60 Robertson Quay) and **The Moomba Tuckshop** (Bank of China Building, 4 Battery Road).

Entrust yourself into the hands of Magdalene Tang at **Mag's Wine Kitchen** (86 Circular Road), an intimate restaurant where daily specials and a magnificent wine cellar are the order of the day. **Peach Garden**'s (OCBC Centre, 65 Chulia Street) excellent *dim sum*, coupled

THIS PAGE (CLOCKWISE FROM TOP): Enjoy classic Japanese fine-dining at KŌ; Peranakan delicacies such as pineapple tarts are a speciality of the InterContinental Singapore; My Humble House is famed for its award-winning Chinese cuisine; Jusman So has made his mark on the Singapore dining scene with reinvented classics such as pan-seared foie gras at Sage, The Restaurant.

OPPOSITE (FROM TOP): Singapore Sling— a trademark cocktail of the island; relax and unwind at New Asia bar at Swissôtel The Stamford.

PAGE 74: Woo that special someone with a romantic stroll along Boat Quay at dusk.

with a panoramic view, makes it a power-lunch favourite. Local talent Jusman So's **Sage, The Restaurant** (7 Mohammed Sultan Road) may be a recent entrant in the food scene, but it has already earned a reputation as a popular dining choice.

bars + cafés

Clubbers are spoilt for choice with some of the best nightlife spots packed within the quays. **Brussels Sprouts** (80 Mohammed Sultan Road) specialises in Belgian beers along with fine pub-grub. **Café Iguana**

(Riverside Point) is known for its Mexican food and margaritas, while **Brewerkz** (Riverside Point) is famed for its beer, brewed on the premises by a microbrewery.

WineGarage's (Riverside Point) extensive wine list is best complemented by its refined menu, especially the Sunday specials. Other notable names in the area include **Helipad**, **The Clinic**, **The Rupee Room**, **Attica** and **Attica Too**, and **supperclub**.

Enjoy a Singapore Sling at the **Long Bar** (Raffles Hotel), the place where the drink was first concocted.

For single malts and cognacs, sister establishment the **Bar & Billiard Room** (Raffles Hotel) is the best choice.

Relax to soothing music at **Naumi Bar** (Naumi Hotel, 41 Seah Street) or sit back with a drink and watch the bartender-magician dazzle at **Bar 84** (Gallery Hotel).

JAZZ@SOUTHBRIDGE (82b Boat Quay) boasts live jazz every day of the week, featuring international musicians and an in-house band, not to mention an extensive selection of whiskies from around the world.

intercontinental singapore

THIS PAGE: *One of the hotel's signature Shophouse Suites, which are decorated in a wholly Peranakan style.*

OPPOSITE (FROM TOP): *Spacious, elegant and light-filled, the brand new Club Lounge at InterContinental Singapore is the ideal private enclave for discerning travellers; the fountain in the driveway welcomes guests to the hotel.*

Rising from the convergence of mainland Chinese immigrants and the European and indigenous people already living on the island of Singapore, the Peranakan—whose men are referred to as Baba and the women, Nyonya—cultivated their own unique style. Today, remnants of Peranakan culture can be seen in the island's surviving shophouses. These are sometimes converted into funky boutiques, small classy restaurants or cosy little cafés. More rarely though, they are refurbished into five-star luxury hotels, such as the InterContinental Singapore.

InterContinental Singapore adopted the shophouses along Malay and Malabar Streets and turned them into cosy guestrooms. Each air-conditioned guestroom has a view of the quaint, covered shopping streets from a private balcony. Inside, the rooms are filled with Peranakan-style furnishings, such as framed tiles, intricate bed headboards and tea chests carved with auspicious phoenix and peony motifs. Other rooms, though not actually located in old Peranakan shophouses, keep to the Straits Chinese theme with ornate lacquer cupboards and Oriental lamps. The public areas of the hotel are unique, featuring wooden ceilings, tiled flooring and white balustrades harking back to the colonial days.

In the heart of the Civic District and up the road from the Central Business District, InterContinental Singapore is a business

rooms
403, including Shophouse Rooms and Suites, the Presidential Suite, luxury suites, 189 Deluxe Rooms, 32 Premier Rooms and 100 Club InterContinental Rooms

food
Olive Tree: international • KŌ: Japanese • Man Fu Yuan Chinese Restaurant: Cantonese • Aroma: pastries, sandwiches • Lobby Lounge: afternoon high tea

drink
Victoria Bar • Aqua Bar: pool bar • Lobby Lounge • Aroma: tea and coffee

features
pool • gym • massage • roof garden • sauna • jacuzzi • function rooms • business centre • Grand Ballroom • meeting rooms • concierge • Club InterContinental concierge services

nearby
Bugis Street • Peranakan Museum • Suntec Singapore International Convention and Exhibition Centre • Little India • Arab Street • Bugis Junction • Bugis MRT station

contact
80 Middle Road, Singapore 188966 • telephone: +65.6338 7600 • facsimile: +65.6338 7366 • email: singapore@interconti.com • website: www.singapore.intercontinental.com

hotel. Club InterContinental guests are able to use the hotel's extensive facilities. With a Club guestroom comes access to the Club floor, where tea and coffee are available all day long, along with breakfast, afternoon tea, evening cocktails and concierge services. In the rooms, guests can pamper themselves with luxury amenities. The Club InterContinental Lounge, which is also a tribute to Peranakan culture, has timber flooring, elegant furniture and a collection of unique art and artefacts, and is equipped with the latest technology needed for work or to keep up with the times. There is also a well-stocked library filled with books on local topics, business and, of course, the Peranakan culture and lifestyle.

It's not all business though; the rooms are so unique that they make for an interesting holiday, offering an insight to some local traditions. In tune with the local heritage, InterContinental Singapore also organises tours showcasing the Peranakan lifestyle.

As for dining options, Olive Tree serves international cuisine, while KŌ is the hotel's Japanese restaurant. Man Fu Yuan is a Cantonese restaurant with six private dining rooms, making it ideal for business lunches or dinners. The Victoria Bar has an extensive beer menu, promising to help tired businessmen relax and unwind, and Aroma is great for a light meal with fresh coffee and tea along with pastries and sandwiches.

While business hotels generally tend to blend in with the crowd, InterContinental Singapore stands out. Proud of its history and heritage, which is evident everywhere from the ballroom to its dedicated service, this is a hotel with a distinct personality.

swissôtel the stamford

Designed by IM Pei, Swissôtel The Stamford, which opened for business in 1986, is one of the tallest hotels in Southeast Asia. Indeed, the top floors of this landmark hotel overlook the skyline of Singapore, up to Malaysia and over the water to Indonesia.

Swissôtel The Stamford's central location and height made it a vantage point during the first Singapore Grand Prix night race in 2008, and will provide the same advantage for future events of a similar nature. The hotel's cylindrical design allows each room to have a panoramic view—as an added bonus, each comes with a personal balcony. Considering there are 1,261 rooms and suites, that's plenty to go around.

Inside, each room is well-appointed, well-maintained and spacious. Broadband Internet is available in every room, and public areas of the hotel offer wireless Internet access.

It is when one arrives at the Stamford Crest that things really step up. A hotel within a hotel, the 64th through to 66th floors are home to 29 suites. These vast and luxurious spaces measuring 70 sq m (750 sq ft) offer the best in hospitality—from exclusive check-in counters to an en-suite bathroom with a flat-screen television, from Bulgari amenities to an iPod docking station and BOSE sound system. Catching up with work away from home is easy with complimentary access to Internet stations

THIS PAGE (FROM TOP): *New Asia is ideal for having drinks with friends or dancing the night away to great music; the Classic Harbour View room offers its guests a sweeping view of Marina Bay and the city's skyline.*

OPPOSITE (FROM TOP): *The view through massive floor-to-ceiling windows enhances the flavour of the fare served at the Equinox Restaurant; the hotel has two pools where guests may enjoy a brisk swim after a long, stressful day.*

rooms
1,261 rooms and suites

food
Jaan: southern French nouvelle •
Kopi Tiam: authentic local • Café Swiss: Swiss •
Equinox Restaurant: Asian and Western •
Out of the Pan: waffles and crêpes

drink
New Asia: cocktails • Introbar: cocktails •
City Space: lounge • Lobby Court: speciality
drinks and hot beverages

features
tallest hotel in Singapore • spa • fitness club •
2 outdoor pools • 6 tennis courts •
business centre • 27 meeting rooms •
Raffles City Convention Centre

nearby
Central Business District • Singapore River •
Parliament • Raffles City Shopping Centre •
Boat Quay • Clarke Quay • CHIJMES •
Esplanade—Theatres on the Bay •
Singapore Art Museum • Suntec Singapore
International Convention and Exhibition Centre

contact
2 Stamford Road, Singapore 178882 •
telephone: +65.6338 8585 •
facsimile: +65.6338 2862 •
email: singapore-stamford@swissotel.com •
website: www.swissotel.com/singapore-
stamford

and exclusive use of meeting rooms. The in-room Lavazza coffee machine is also of great help during late nights. Furthermore, guests of Stamford Crest can enjoy all-day coffee, tea and cookies and exclusive use of the Living Room, where daily breakfasts and evening cocktails are served. They may even utilise the Private Fitness Centre and Willow Stream Spa.

Business travellers may also want to consider the alternative option of staying in Swiss Executive Club rooms. In addition to other perks, guests staying in these rooms have access to the spa, evening cocktails in the lounge, iPod docking stations and coffee machines in each room. The adjacent technologically-advanced Raffles City Convention Centre provides an amazing 6,500 sq m (70,000 sq ft) of meeting space and boasts a satellite conference system for global conferencing.

A remarkable collection of 16 restaurants and bars is scattered throughout the hotel, and the Equinox Complex is home to five of them. After starting on the ground floor with Introbar, the lift whizzes you up to New Asia on the 71st floor, with floor-to-ceiling windows and impressive views. Down one level is the Equinox Restaurant, loved for its champagne Sunday brunches. The food is a combination of Asian and Western cuisines. Also on the 70th floor, Jaan serves southern French nouvelle cuisine while City Space is perfect for after-dinner drinks. Private dining rooms are available for power-lunches and other functions.

A businessman's playground, Raffles City Shopping Centre is just downstairs, so guests may partake of the national pastime at their leisure. Alternatively, an evening at the riverside is only a 10-minute walk away.

the fullerton hotel singapore

The Fullerton Hotel Singapore is an exquisite blend of tradition and modernity. It is a magnificent structure that preserves the island-state's rich colonial history while offering its guests a luxurious stay and access to everything modern Singapore has to offer.

Completed in 1928, the building that houses The Fullerton Hotel Singapore was once home to the General Post Office, the Chamber of Commerce and the Singapore Club. It was later converted into a five-star luxury hotel. The Fullerton Hotel Singapore is an example of Palladian architecture, with tall Doric columns and grand *porte-cochères*. The hotel's interior is stylish and contemporary, yet still pays homage to its architectural roots with motifs that date back to 1928. The lobby's high ceiling creates an impression of limitless space, while contemporary art pieces provide an Asian touch at this Singaporean landmark.

Here in the hotel, there are a total of 400 rooms and suites which either overlook the sunlit atrium courtyard or provide their inhabitants with stunning views of the river promenade, downtown Singapore's skyline or the sea. In addition, all bathrooms are equipped with sleek, streamlined fittings and luxurious bathroom amenities.

The crème de la crème of The Fullerton Hotel Singapore's accommodations is the lavish 199-sq m (2,142-sq ft) Presidential Suite, which is accessed through its own private elevator. The Suite's glass-enclosed verandah provides an ideal location for private dinners.

THIS PAGE (FROM TOP): Guests can indulge in an array of tasty Chinese dishes at Jade; relax by the pool after a long day of sightseeing or work.

OPPOSITE (FROM TOP): The Governor Suite is one of the 28 opulent suites available to guests; located at the mouth of the Singapore River, the hotel is a welcoming sight for boats entering the city.

...an exquisite blend of tradition and modernity.

Designed with the business and leisure traveller in mind, the hotel offers facilities that cater to both. There is a 24-hour Financial Centre with full business support services and workstations with high-speed Internet access. For leisure, there is an outdoor infinity-edge pool, 24-hour fitness centre and The Asian Spa.

Apart from The Courtyard—the lobby lounge which serves afternoon tea and offers a selection of premium blends and beverages, and live classical music—the hotel also hosts several restaurants that specialise in different types of food. Guests can savour international dishes in a smart-casual setting at Town Restaurant, modern Chinese specialities at Jade and Italian cuisine at the fine-dining restaurant San Marco at The Lighthouse.

The hotel's prime location in Raffles Place is at the intersection of Singapore's business, financial and cultural districts. Theatres, a concert hall, a museum and the Raffles Place Mass Rapid Transit (MRT) station are within walking distance. Boat Quay and Clarke Quay, major dining and entertainment districts, are only a stroll away. The hotel's premier location also made it a coveted address during the Formula One Grand Prix in Singapore.

Its host of modern facilities, thoughtful amenities and personalised service has won The Fullerton Hotel Singapore major distinctions such as a place in the *Condé Nast Traveler* Gold List and *Travel + Leisure*'s World's Best Awards. It has also been voted by readers of *Condé Nast Traveler* as the Best Hotel in Asia.

rooms
372 rooms · 28 suites

food
Town Restaurant: international ·
San Marco at The Lighthouse: modern Italian ·
The Courtyard: lobby lounge ·
Jade: fine Chinese

drink
Post Bar: wine, martinis and signature cocktails

features
outdoor infinity-edge pool · jogging route ·
24-hour fitness centre · limousine hire ·
disabled access · luxury boutiques ·
babysitting service · 9 meeting rooms ·
24-hour full-service business office ·
high-speed wireless Internet access

nearby
business district · Boat Quay · Clarke Quay ·
Esplanade—Theatres on the Bay · museum

contact
1 Fullerton Square, Singapore 049178 ·
telephone: +65.6733 8388 ·
facsimile: +65.6735 8388 ·
email: info@fullertonhotel.com ·
website: www.fullertonhotel.com

the ritz-carlton, millenia singapore

THIS PAGE (FROM TOP): *An exotic dish of braised crocodile skin is served at Summer Pavilion; the premier suite is one of the many spacious, luxurious and comfortable options offered.*

OPPOSITE (FROM LEFT): *The Chihuly Lounge is an elegant setting in which guests can indulge in a cocktail, a glass of champagne or a refined afternoon tea; even while enjoying a long, romantic bath, guests can take in lovely views of the city.*

Absolutely no expense was spared to create The Ritz-Carlton, Millenia Singapore, one of the most lavish and modern hotels in the city-state; its breathtaking architecture is the work of Pritzker Prize-winner Kevin Roche. The hotel houses an astonishing 4,200-piece modern art collection, which includes masterpieces by such renowned artists as Frank Stella, Andy Warhol and Dale Chihuly.

The Ritz-Carlton, Millenia Singapore's location and design was planned with the intent of providing spectacular views from every room. All of the hotel's guestrooms and bathrooms offer stunning panoramas of either Marina Bay or Kallang Bay and the city skyline. Each of the oversized rooms is also appointed as a modern lap of luxury, featuring large marble-tiled bathrooms with octagonal windows, decadent European bath amenities, high-speed Internet access, plush furniture and spacious walk-in wardrobes.

At the top of The Ritz-Carlton, Millenia Singapore is the prestigious Ritz-Carlton Club, which comprises 128 club rooms, including 19 one-bedroom suites, three two-bedroom suites and The Ritz-Carlton Suite.

Guests of The Ritz-Carlton Club enjoy a dedicated concierge service, complimentary Internet access, a private Club Lounge where culinary and beverage presentations—also complimentary—are served, and comfortable rooms that feature feather beds with fluffy goose-down duvets, flat-screen televisions, DVD players and personal butler service.

Foodies will be spoilt for choice here at The Ritz-Carlton, Millenia Singapore. The Summer Pavilion, which is set in a peaceful Suzhou rock garden, is the hotel's signature restaurant. It serves traditional Cantonese cuisine in a modern setting.

The all-day restaurant, Greenhouse, features food influenced by international cuisines. Large enough to seat up to 240 guests at any one time, Greenhouse has established itself as Singapore's premier Sunday champagne brunch destination.

In addition, the Chihuly Lounge offers afternoon tea, while cocktails and champagne may be enjoyed throughout the day.

Conference facilities include the vast 1,094-sq m (11,781-sq ft) Grand Ballroom with its state-of-the-art audio-visual and lighting equipment, the stylish Chihuly Room and 11 meeting and function rooms.

The fitness centre and spa is the perfect place to work out or unwind after a long day. The Spa boasts a unique Chocolate De-Ager treatment—a bath of warmed chocolate mixed with sweet almond oil—that utilises the anti-aging properties of cocoa.

The Ritz-Carlton, Millenia Singapore provides one of the finest hotel experiences in Asia and has developed a reputation for impeccable service. In addition to equally prestigious accolades, the hotel was rated as Best Hotel in Singapore by *Asiamoney* and listed as one of the Top 50 Hotels in Asia by *Travel + Leisure* in 2007 and 2008.

...provides one of the finest hotel experiences in Asia.

rooms
608 rooms • 19 one-bedroom suites •
3 two-bedroom suites • 1 Ritz-Carlton suite

food
Summer Pavilion: Cantonese •
Greenhouse: international

drink
Chihuly Lounge • Pool Bar

features
babysitting • gift shop • florist • fitness centre •
spa • technology butler • limousine pickup •
executive business services • high-speed
Internet access • meeting rooms

nearby
business and financial district • civic and
cultural district • shopping • theatre •
museums • bars and clubs • dining •
sightseeing • city tour • Singapore Flyer

contact
7 Raffles Avenue, Singapore 039799 •
telephone: +65.6337 8888 •
facsimile: +65.6338 0001 •
email: rc.sinrz.reservations@ritzcarlton.com •
website: www.ritzcarlton.com/hotels/singapore

garibaldi group of restaurants

THIS PAGE: *Garibaldi was the first of the group's establishments.*

OPPOSITE (FROM TOP): *Chef Galetti is the culinary genius behind the group's authentic cuisine; DeSté produces chocolate that is used exclusively in its line of desserts, including this dish, known as Italian Garden.*

For a relatively new group, Garibaldi Group's success story is something of a marvel. And the signs are that its growth is far from over. New and exciting concepts are springing from this group at a regular pace, providing Singapore with the finer things in life in all packages, from fine dining to casual dining, from gourmet retail to bar-bistros. Closely associated to the group, Gunther's and Brotzeit are also not to be missed; the former serves French cuisine and the latter, authentic German fare and beer.

The group's first establishment was Garibaldi, helmed by Chef de Cuisine Roberto Galetti. With 20 years of restaurant experience gained throughout the world, including some time at Bice restaurant in Buenos Aires and the

Four Seasons Hotel in Tokyo, Chef Galetti was well qualified to bring Italian fine dining to Singapore. Garibaldi's specialities include spanner crab salad with avocado and angel hair pasta with lobster, sweet peas and tomato sauce. For dessert the *cannolo sicilliano*, filled with ricotta cheese, chocolate chips and pistachio nuts, is a sublime interpretation of the traditional recipe. The restaurant is a showcase of class and style, and its food and ambience, as well as its dedication to authenticity, has turned this into one of Singapore's most popular and well-respected fine-dining establishments.

Riding on the success of Garibaldi, Ricciotti Pizza, Pasta & Deli provides the same standard of Italian food but in a more casual setting. Attention to décor is still evident—leather seats the colour of dark chocolate, marble flooring and wooden tabletops give the restaurant a modern edge. On the menu are favourites such as pizza, pasta, panini and salads, as well as meat and fish dishes. The many pastries, cakes and gourmet food on offer at the deli counter are also quite an attraction. There are two branches of Ricciotti Pizza, Pasta & Deli, one on the river between Boat Quay and Clarke Quay and one in the Central Business District. The latter buzzes with activity during the week, when corporate types take advantage of the set lunch, while the weekends tend to be quieter.

Gelato, pastries, cakes and *petits fours* have always been an important part of the Garibaldi Group restaurants and now they have their very own confectionery-cum-pastry laboratory-cum-retail-store. DeSté is the newest kid on the Garibaldi block and promises to be something of a groundbreaker here in Singapore. Stefano Deiuri is a fifth generation pastry chef who hails from Italy; he promises extravagant, one-of-a-kind and unparalleled dishes, with chocolate at the core of his sweet gastronomic creations. The chef can make cakes to order and his team come up with new confections every day in their state-of-the-art lab.

For a selection of well-thought out and well-executed menus that can be savoured in contemporary settings, you can't really go wrong with any of the restaurants that make up the Garibaldi group. In fact, you can expect nothing less than the highest quality and absolute authenticity.

seats
Garibaldi: 100, 3 private rooms • Ricciotti Pizza, Pasta & Deli, The Riverwalk: 100 • Ricciotti Pizza, Pasta & Deli, China Square Central: 65

food
Garibaldi: Italian fine dining • Ricciotti Pizza, Pasta & Deli: Italian casual dining • DeSté: confectionery, patisserie

drink
Garibaldi: Italian wine • Ricciotti Pizza, Pasta & Deli: Italian wine

features
Garibaldi: valet parking • DeSté: gourmet patisserie, chocolates, corporate gifts

contact
Garibaldi: 36 Purvis Street, #01-02, Singapore 188613 • telephone: +65.6837 1468 •

Ricciotti Pizza, Pasta & Deli, The Riverwalk: 20 Upper Circular Road, #B1-49/50 The Riverwalk, Singapore 058416 • telephone: +65.6533 9060 •

Ricciotti Pizza, Pasta & Deli, China Square Central: 3 Pickering Street, #01-36/37 Nankin Row, China Square Central, Singapore 048660 • telephone: +65.6438 8040 •

DeSté: 20 Upper Circular Road, #01-39/41 The Riverwalk, Singapore 058416 • telephone: +65.6536 1556 •

website: www.garibaldigroup.com.sg

gunther's

THIS PAGE: *The lights inside the restaurant are focused on the tables to highlight the food.*

OPPOSITE (FROM TOP): *The chef's talent and skill are evident after the very first mouthful; the chef's speciality—cold angel's hair pasta truffle scented with oscietra caviar— not only looks enticingly delicious, it also tastes great.*

Gunther Hubrechsen's CV reads like a perfect record of fine dining finesse; so pristine, you might worry that expectations are set too high. But fear not, the chef delivers one of the best dining experiences that can be found here in the city-state of Singapore.

Having trained at the Bruges Culinary Institute Voor Voeding (IVV), Gunther worked at Alain Passard's famed L' Arpege in Paris, a three Michelin-starred institution where he started as a trainee and ended as sous-chef. When he arrived in Singapore in 2002 it was to lead the famed establishment, Les Amis, to a higher standing. This he achieved, attaining the rank of 83 in the prestigious *Restaurant* magazine's World's Best 100. After five years in Singapore, Gunther teamed up with the Garibaldi group to set up his eponymous restaurant. And it is here that he has found his home, a place where he can concentrate on his unfussy and sublime menu.

Just a short distance from Raffles Hotel, on the swanky Purvis Street—home to many a high-end furniture brand and partner,

Garibaldi restaurant—Gunther's may seem unassuming at first sight. Upon entering the champagne bar the maître d' ushers you into the deceptively large restaurant; it can seat 50 patrons at once. The walls are dark, the feel is sophisticated, and the overall effect is modern and urban chic. The clever lighting keeps diners in an enticing murkiness but gives the table centre stage with the food firmly in the spotlight. This was the intention, so that the food remains the most important feature.

When it comes to the menu, Gunther's style is pure, elegant and progressive; the presentation perfect, the French cuisine innovative. At the same time, dishes are not convoluted, letting the purity of the top-quality ingredients speak for itself. The chef has a flair for using natural *jus* and slow cooking techniques to enhance the flavour of the food. This is not an easy thing to get right, as stripping down the food in this manner makes it easier to detect mistakes. But this is not a problem for Chef Gunther. With a firm focus on using only the best quality ingredients, the menu changes on a quarterly basis with the seasons.

Gunther's ability and outright talent is evident throughout. Take his specialities—confit of egg, cold angel hair pasta truffle scented with oscietra caviar, *côte de bœuf* with confit of onion and grilled sea bass with rice pilaf—all are executed with a gift for reinterpreting classic dishes and a delicate sensitivity that ensures that every ingredient's

full potential is expressed. Vegetarians will be pleased to hear that Chef Gunther's skill with vegetables is extraordinary; he turns ordinary vegetables into dishes that are able to stand on their own, the salt-baked beetroot with grilled mushrooms being just one example of this. Signature desserts at Gunther's include the apple tart, the warm champagne sabayon and the Valronha's Manjari chocolate fondant with ice cream, each one an exquisite end to an unforgettable meal.

In all, this is a restaurant not to be missed. Expect fine dining in every sense, from the ambience to the service and most of all the genuinely superb food. But be sure to book in advance; Gunther's tables have been full every night since it opened, and it shows no sign of losing its popularity. Without a doubt, this is a gourmet spot with staying power.

seats
50 • 2 private dining rooms for up to 24

food
modern French

drink
champagne bar • extensive wine list

features
catering for private events • special events

nearby
Raffles City Shopping Centre • Raffles Hotel • Suntec Singapore International Convention and Exhibition Centre • Civic District

contact
36 Purvis Street, #01-03, Singapore 188613 • telephone: +65.6338 8955 • facsimile: +65.6337 3770 • email: restaurant@gunthers.com.sg • website: www.gunthers.com.sg

my humble house

My Humble House turns Chinese food into haute cuisine with its blend of Western accents and traditional Chinese cooking techniques. Located in Singapore's theatre complex, the Esplanade Mall, the restaurant provides diners with stunning views of the Singapore River. Inside, the über-trendy décor makes this institution an absolute must-try for the chichi crowd who want something a bit more special.

Every inch of the restaurant exhibits an artistic flair. The seats, with extended out-of-proportion backs, are covered with eclectic fabric such as cowhide or suede. As a Chinese establishment, the use of rosewood and teak is not surprising, but with elements of modern décor, the restaurant's look is fresh and progressive. The 'intelligent' lighting, designed by Kuro Mende, is adjusted for each time of the day with the use of fibre optics and clever light features. Also, interior architect Antonio Eraso has crafted a space that is at once unique and modern—the feel is that of an elegant private home with a welcoming cosiness. All in all, these form the perfect backdrop for an inspired menu.

THIS PAGE (FROM TOP): *Tender wagyu beef is a treat for the taste buds and a work of art; an illuminated pillar draped with strings of crystals stands proudly in the bar area.*

OPPOSITE (FROM TOP): *The sleek interior of the restaurant is ideal for corporate functions; foie gras is not traditionally a part of Chinese cuisine, but My Humble House prepares it so well that it doesn't matter.*

As a running theme, the 'art of dining' applies to the menu as much as to the décor, and presentation is one of the key features of My Humble House. This is evident right from the start with whimsical dish names, such as Dance of the Wind, Sauntering Among the Golden Leaves and A Duet, For Love, For Life, and set menu titles which range from Someone is Singing Behind the Mountain to The Delicate Snow Fell at Midnight.

The team, led by the group's Corporate Chef and Director of Kitchens Sam Leong, puts great effort into translating art into food, and their hard work has certainly borne fruit. The execution is perfect; the flavours are well combined and the look follows through with genuine gastronomic delight. The house specialities include crisp-fried oysters glazed with champagne mousse—take note of the Western accent that comes with the presence of champagne—the double-boiled seafood *consommé* served in a coconut, and the seafood crispy rice in green tea broth that has a distinctly Chinese twist.

Perhaps its biggest achievement aside from its staying power—amazing in a city like Singapore where restaurants come and go with the fickle crowd—is My Humble House's listing as one of The World's 100 Best Restaurants by the survey of the prestigious London-based magazine, *Restaurant*. Readers may be interested to know that this exclusive list names only two Chinese restaurants, which makes My Humble House part of an

elite crowd. The restaurant's other accolades include being listed as one of the Top 10 Romantic Spots in Singapore.

A stylish venue for private parties, corporate functions and other such events, My Humble House has a separate dining room where guests can conduct smaller, more intimate gatherings in a quiet space. Another unique feature is the kitchen encased in rose-tinted glass, where the skilled chefs perform their magic.

In touch with its roots, the food served here remains distinctly Chinese. However, with a modern approach and a readiness to introduce new flavours, the adventurous chefs deliver tasty creations that are completely new and unusual—Singapore's definitive answer to modern Chinese cuisine.

seats
80 • 1 private dining room for 13

food
contemporary Chinese

drink
a wide variety of wine • champagne and cocktails

features
glass-encased open kitchen • weddings • 'art of dining' concept • designer lighting • corporate and private functions

nearby
Esplanade–Theatres on the Bay

contact
8 Raffles Avenue,
#02-27/29 Esplanade Mall,
Singapore 039802 •
telephone: +65.6423 1881 •
facsimile: +65.6423 1551 •
email: myhumblehouse@tunglok.com •
website: www.myhumblehouse.com.sg

peach garden chinese restaurants

THIS PAGE: *Peach Garden @ 33 features many large windows which showcase the view that draws many to the restaurant.*

OPPOSITE (FROM TOP): *Due to the chefs' efforts, each offering brought to the table is as tasty as it is visually appealing; the restaurants are ideal venues for weddings and other private or corporate functions.*

The peach has long been a symbol of purity in China, where peach orchards have featured in pivotal myths and legends throughout the ages. Similarly, the Peach Garden name has come to represent the essence of Chinese cuisine in Singapore, and connotes a singularly satisfying dining experience. Popular among connoisseurs and prominent members of the business elite, the three restaurants of the Peach Garden group—and the new outlet at Orchid Country Club that will open in 2009—place equal emphasis on service and culinary excellence, earning every bit of their celebrated status.

Peach Garden was started in 2002 by industry veterans Angela Ho and Veronica Tan, each bringing to this new venture close to 30 years of experience obtained in some of the country's best dining halls. The first restaurant opened in Novena Gardens, a relatively quiet residential neighbourhood, about 10 minutes from the shops of bustling Orchard Road.

With the assistance of a master chef from Hong Kong and an experienced management team, the restaurant soon earned a reputation for authentic Cantonese cuisine enhanced with modern cooking techniques. By the time the second restaurant opened in Thomson Plaza in 2005, fan favourites such as fried prawns with *wasabi* mayonnaise and pan-fried sea perch fillets in plum sauce were already established as signature dishes of their menu.

The Peach Garden secret involves taking traditional dishes such as roasted golden suckling pig and double-boiled shark bone soup, and preparing them to perfection before presenting them in style. This offers entirely new contexts in which to view familiar dishes. The emphasis on quality ingredients in the kitchen extends beyond using the highest grade of regionally grown produce. Many components are painstakingly sourced for authenticity—*hor fun* noodles (wide Chinese noodles made from rice) are brought in from Ipoh, Malaysia, while preserved Chinese sausage and orange peels are sourced from Hong Kong. The result is a collection of flavours that spans the Chinese diaspora; these are then ingeniously combined with Western accents.

In 2007, a third restaurant opened in the downtown business district. The Peach Garden @ 33 in The Executives' Club is located, as its name suggests, on the 33rd floor of OCBC Centre on Chulia Street. Warm, inviting and elegantly furnished, the Oriental dining hall is spacious enough to host large events, and yet clever table placement makes every meal feel like a private event.

Apart from the impeccable *dim sum* creations of the Master Chef and his team, Peach Garden @ 33 offers the added perk of an

extraordinary panoramic view over the city and waterfront. Stretching across the famed Esplanade—Theatres on the Bay structure and other landmarks, this scenery provides visitors to the restaurant's Bar Lounge area with a unique backdrop for light snacks in the day and a full range of drinks by night.

An additional service that Peach Garden provides is catering for private or corporate events. Now Peach Garden's signature dishes can be enjoyed even at home.

Just as tales were spun of China's legendary peach gardens, so too have Peach Garden's accomplishments been recognised in the pages of *Singapore Tatler*, *Wine & Dine* and *The Peak*. Still, it's a safe bet that the ancients missed out on prawns in *wasabi* mayonnaise.

seats
Novena Gardens: 140, 4 private rooms •
Thomson Plaza: 300, 9 private rooms •
Peach Garden @ 33: 230, 10 private rooms

food
traditional and modern Cantonese • *dim sum*

drink
Bar Lounge (at the Peach Garden @ 33)

features
catering • weddings • functions

contact
Peach Garden @ Novena Gardens:
273 Thomson Road, #01-06 Novena Gardens,
Singapore 307644 •
telephone: +65.6254 3383 •
facsimile: +65.6254 4633 •

Peach Garden @ Thomson Plaza:
301 Upper Thomson Road,
#01-88 Thomson Plaza, Singapore 574408 •
telephone: +65.6451 3233 •
facsimile: +65.6451 0509 •

Peach Garden @ 33 in The Executives' Club:
65 Chulia Street, #33-01 OCBC Centre,
Singapore 049513 •
telephone: +65.6535 7833 •
facsimile: +65.6532 6733 •

email: catering@peachgarden.com.sg •
website: www.peachgarden.com.sg

saint pierre

Saint Pierre is headed by vivacious Belgian Chef Emmanuel Stroobant, a chef who has passion in spades. It was his passion that drove him from a dishwashing job, at the age of 16, up through the ranks of Belgium's best restaurants. Once fine dining got into this young man's blood, university and studying law were left behind. Clearly, Chef Stroobant chose the right path.

Chef Stroobant's first restaurant opened in Belgium when he was just 23. A storming success, he then moved to Australia to leave his mark on the other side of the world. After five years down under, he shifted to Kuala Lumpur, in Malaysia. This was the defining watershed in Chef Stroobant's life. Immersing himself in the local culture and determined to get to grips with the Malaysian palate, Chef Stroobant was on a mission. He succeeded— World Asia Media named him Best Executive Chef in 1999. That same year saw the chef and his wife move south to Singapore. The year 2000 saw the opening of Saint Pierre, and they haven't looked back since.

Right from its inception, the menu at Saint Pierre has changed every quarter. Chef Stroobant's creativity shines through with every innovation. Guests can be sure of a new

THIS PAGE (FROM TOP): Garnished with great care and attention to detail, each dish is sure to be both aesthetically pleasing and a treat for the palate; Chef Stroobant bestows the finishing touch to each dish to ensure that it is perfect before it is served to a patron.

OPPOSITE: The best caviar, lobster and tuna, among other ingredients, come together to become innovative creations.

Chef Stroobant's creativity shines through with every innovation.

seats
60 · private rooms for 12 and 14

food
modern French

drink
extensive wine list · champagne

features
foie gras menu · degustation menu

nearby
The Riverside Piazza · Riverside Point ·
Central Square · Clarke Quay · Merchant Square

contact
3 Magazine Road, #01-01 Central Mall,
Singapore 059570 ·
telephone: +65.6438 0887 ·
facsimile: +65.6438 4887 ·
email: info@saintpierre.com.sg ·
website: www.saintpierre.com.sg

experience every time they visit. Of course, the signature dishes are constant. These include pan-fried *foie gras* with caramelised apple and old port sauce, braised black cod in white miso with warm Japanese eggplant salad and Shiraz dressing, and homemade flourless Belgian chocolate cake with strawberry coulis and ice cream. A feature unique to Saint Pierre is its separate *foie gras* menu offering six methods of preparation. Two are a constant presence—the signature and a terrine which is garnished differently according to the freshest ingredients available—while the other four vary from season to season.

Another special feature, a true feather in Saint Pierre's cap, is its coveted membership in the Relais and Chateaux group. The only establishment in Singapore to be a member, the restaurant was selected because of Chef Stroobant's "unfailingly innovative, complex and sophisticated" cuisine. If this praise is not enough to entice, a look at the finer details will surely convince you that a meal here is well worth it. For a start, Chef Stroobant and his wife Edina make sure that every member of the floor staff is trained well and informed of every dish (no mean feat). As a result, the discreet and expert staff have added to the restaurant's glowing reputation. The private dining rooms also make this an ideal venue for a business lunch to impress, with the five-course lunch tailored for just this purpose. The wine list is compiled with a fine touch and an eye for flavour, and there are no less than 14 labels available by the glass.

Overall though, this restaurant is famous for its innovative cuisine. Saint Pierre's leading status lies in Chef Stroobant's ingenious flair for amazing cuisine that piques the interest of customers and keeps them coming back.

si chuan dou hua restaurants

THIS PAGE: Each type of premium Chinese tea on the menu has unique properties and affects one's health differently as compared to the others.

OPPOSITE (FROM LEFT): One of the private dining rooms where corporate functions or small, intimate dinners can be held; enjoy a tasty dish of sliced pork with garlic and chilli.

Consider China's great exports, those that changed history and brought the world's attention to her doorstep, and invariably two will emerge as the most culturally significant: tea drinking and Chinese cuisine. Certain kinds of tea are more highly prized than others, and the same can be said for the other—the province of Szechuan is credited for being the home of China's culinary soul, its food full of fire and robust flavours, with Cantonese recipes coming a close second.

The Si Chuan Dou Hua Restaurant group combines these elements in each of its exemplary dining establishments. Over the past 12 years, it has become synonymous with the pairing of fine Chinese meals and the highest grade of Chinese teas available anywhere on the island. Both Szechuanese and Cantonese cuisines are represented, the latter in the form of a *dim sum* menu with 100 unique items. The first restaurant's success led to the opening of another Singapore address, two authentic teahouse concept restaurants and overseas branches in Kuala Lumpur and Tokyo. The second local restaurant has the additional distinction of being Singapore's highest Chinese restaurant with its location on the top floor of UOB Plaza in the downtown business district. Recently, Si Chuan Dou Hua Restaurant was invited to participate in the 2008 World Gourmet Summit, showcasing its specialities in the company of some of the most influential chefs and restauranteurs worldwide.

Although Szechuan cuisine is renowned for being extremely spicy, there are actually 30 distinct flavours recognised by Szechuan master chefs. All these flavours can be found in the creations of Executive Chef Zeng Feng. A veteran with over 25 years of experience and recognition as an 'Advanced-Grade Master Chef' by the Chinese government, his complex and satisfying food forms the backbone of such buffet events as the 60 Dishes Deluxe Feast and 100 Dim Sum Delights.

The enjoyment of tea with every meal is an essential tenet of the chef's philosophy; every dish should be complemented by one of the more than 25 blends of white, green, red, floral and yellow teas on offer. Just as the Japanese have a tea ceremony, diners here are treated to a performance by a Tea Master. The skills possessed by the Tea Master include the refinement and grace attained only with years of training, as the bronze teapots used feature metre- (3.28 ft-) long spouts. Si Chuan Dou Hua Restaurant has the honour of being one of the few places outside of China with expert Tea Masters, who perform a variety of elegant dances as they serve the precious beverage.

This reverence for tea elevates the brewing process into an art form. In the same spirit, the group created Tian Fu Teahouse, where tea can be enjoyed with light meals, in a traditional setting. Both restaurants now incorporate a Tian Fu Teahouse, so that the full scope of Chinese culinary achievements can be appreciated wherever one chooses to dine.

...synonymous with the pairing of fine Chinese meals and the highest grade of Chinese teas...

seats
Parkroyal on Beach Road: 200 • UOB Plaza: 220

food
Szechuan and Cantonese

drink
over 25 varieties of Chinese tea

features
acrobatic tea servers • private dining rooms •
Tian Fu Teahouses within restaurants •
Imperial High Tea in the afternoons •
100 Dim Sum Delights buffet •
60 Dishes Deluxe Feast

nearby
Central Business District • Orchard Road

contact
Parkroyal on Beach Road:
7500 Beach Road, Singapore 199591 •
telephone: +65.6505 5722 •
facsimile: +65.6298 0716 •
email: douhua@br.parkroyalhotels.com •

UOB Plaza:
80 Raffles Place, #60-01 UOB Plaza 1,
Singapore 048624 •
telephone: +65.6535 6006 •
facsimile: +65.6534 5875 •
email: top@sichuandouhua.com •

website: www.sichuandouhua.com

supperclub

THIS PAGE: Rub shoulders with other trendy club-goers in La Salle Neige while savouring items from the dinner menu.

OPPOSITE (FROM TOP): Enjoy a cocktail or a glass of fine wine with the tasty offerings of Chef van der Zalm's kitchen; Le Bar Rouge, as its name implies, is draped in bold scarlet accented by touches of black, white and silver.

Singapore's ongoing cultural transformation has seen its party scene take some enormous leaps of late. Gone are the staid, cookie-cutter clubs offering tired soundtracks and neutered nightlife events. Recent years have seen the opening of Parisian cabaret clubs and concept bar-restaurants, as well as the birth of a thriving arts scene and the relaxation of operating laws—allowing for longer nights of unfettered hedonism.

With these recent developments, the internationally renowned supperclub group has seen it fit to open its latest enterprise in what was once considered an unlikely place. Joining the supperclub establishments in Amsterdam, San Francisco and Istanbul, in addition to the floating 'supperclub cruise' boat docked in The Netherlands, the newest supperclub—located in Singapore—displays a substantial amount of class and cool; in all likelihood it's the best one yet.

Nestled right in the heart of downtown Singapore, within walking distance of various places of interest such as museums, shopping centres and the legendary Raffles Hotel, supperclub is very easy to find (but not so easy to leave). Patrons gain entrance by passing through a 19th-century façade that exudes majesty, which is decorated with contrasting stainless steel tiles, before the supperclub's main La Salle Neige dining hall is revealed.

True to the supperclub philosophy, this new urban enclave of the unexpected is an ode to freedom—no two nights are ever the same, and most of the usual rules do not apply. Inside its sleek split-level bar area clad in plush white fabrics and ultra-modern white plastics, two long rows of white lounge beds stretch along the walls, and everyone is bathed in light. Gone are the high stools to navigate in the near-darkness—this daring approach seems to bring out the best in clubbers, who mingle freely and come dressed in their boldest outfits.

Chef Ulpho van der Zalm prepares an undisclosed five-course dinner each night, with completely new menus that debut every week. One never knows what to expect of his flavours and presentations, except that they will definitely delight even discerning palates. Those with an insatiable appetite for detail may choose to peek into the open-concept kitchen for an early preview. Over the course of the evening, as diners eat while reclined or sitting cross-legged on the beds, entertainment as unpredictable as the menu unfolds. A steady stream of artists, poets, musicians and performers appear each night, and there's little telling what one might experience during any particular visit. A bit of costumed theatre, an exotic dance or a duet between two improbable instrumentalists—prepare to be surprised.

La Chambre Privee is the club's purple-clad private dining room. It has its own bar counter as well as a large square bed at its centre that splits into four, or rolls away at a moment's notice to create a dance floor for post-dinner partying. More intimate meetings may occur at Le Bar Rouge, a lounge decked in scarlet at one end of La Salle Neige, with darkened windows displaying the city skyline. Over fine wines and signature supper**club** cocktails, be sure to revel in each unique moment, because a whole new experience begins the next time the club's doors open.

seats
restaurant: 250 • club: 600

food
five-course fusion dinner each night, menu changes weekly

drink
cocktails • spirits • wine list

features
nightly performances • bed seating • live DJs • private dining room • smoking room • unisex bathrooms

nearby
Esplanade–Theatres on the Bay • Raffles Hotel • Orchard Road • shopping • museums

contact
331 North Bridge Road, Odeon Towers, Singapore 188720 •
telephone: +65.6334 4080 •
facsimile: +65.6334 4085 •
email: singapore@supperclub.com •
website: www.supperclub.com

true blue cuisine

THIS PAGE (FROM TOP): The dark wood furniture, lanterns and decorations in the main dining hall are pure Straits Chinese; items such as these kebaya (embroidered blouses) are on offer at the True Blue Shoppe.

OPPOSITE (FROM TOP): This dish of minced meat seasoned with Chinese five-spice powder is a popular favourite with locals; the ornaments on the walls of the restaurant add to its vintage, homey atmosphere.

One of the most distinctive elements in the makeup of Singaporean identity, Peranakan culture and cuisine are unique to the island and its surrounding territories. The word 'Peranakan' means 'descendant' in Malay, although they are also known as the Straits Chinese. The story of the Peranakan people began over five centuries ago, when Chinese immigrants integrated with the indigenous communities through intermarriage and the adoption of cultural practices. Peranakan contributions to the culinary landscape of Singapore, Malaysia and the region are significant because they merge Chinese recipes and cooking techniques with the spices and sensibilities of Malay and Indonesian cuisine—in much the same way as their language combines Bahasa Melayu with the Hokkien dialect.

The Peranakan Museum in Singapore, a branch of the Asian Civilisations Museum, was established in 2008 as the world's foremost repository of artefacts chronicling the history of the Straits Chinese people. Since 2003, however, those seeking to immerse themselves in Peranakan culture have sought out another local institution, the True Blue Cuisine restaurant. Originally located in the Katong district, a hotbed of Peranakan activity, the restaurant now occupies a shophouse directly adjacent to the Peranakan Museum, on Armenian Street in central Singapore, giving visitors an opportunity to experience the complete Peranakan story in one visit.

The family-owned restaurant is part living tapestry, part gastronomic time capsule. It achieves this by providing an authentic Peranakan home experience that illustrates the way life was once lived, not in the form of static exhibits, but through actual continuing practice. The air in the central courtyard of the building tingles with the pungent scent of *belachan* (spiced shrimp paste) left to dry in the sun, while throughout the halls and private rooms, *bunga rampay*, an aromatic potpourri of shredded pandan leaves and crushed flowers, leaves a gentle fragrance.

The new dining room on the ground floor seats 60, while three private dining rooms accommodate special celebrations of six, 10 and 20 guests respectively. Antique porcelain, furniture and original photographs decorate each space, providing a personal record of bygone times. Be sure to request for a viewing of the collection of rose-cut diamond jewellery on display in the six-seater private room—a rare treasure by any measure.

Operated by chefs Benjamin Seck, his mother Daisy Seah and cousin Irene Ong, True Blue Cuisine is only one part of the family's campaign to preserve and extend their way of life. A sister company produces traditional handicrafts and embroidered clothing, many of which are available on the premises as souvenirs in the True Blue Shoppe. However,

the dedication of Seck's family to their Peranakan heritage comes through most clearly in the food, prepared according to handwritten recipes passed down from one generation to the next.

In addition to well-known staples such as *laksa*, a curried noodle soup prepared with coconut milk, True Blue Cuisine also bakes a fresh selection of traditional pastries and cakes each day, to be taken home by patrons, or enjoyed on the spot with a classic beverage such as red date tea, or a cool glass of lime juice with basil seeds, lemongrass, and kaffir lime leaves. Visitors who wish to understand Straits Chinese culture should stop by True Blue Cuisine for a cold glass of lime juice and some traditional fare, which will allow him or her to experience a taste of Peranakan life.

seats
dining room: 60 · private rooms for 6, 10 and 20

food
authentic Peranakan

drink
traditional Peranakan teas and lime juices

features
airwell · collection of artefacts · gift shop

nearby
Peranakan Museum · The Substation · Singapore Philatelic Museum

contact
47/49 Armenian Street, Singapore 179937 · telephone: +65.6440 0449 · facsimile: +65.6440 3358 · email: info@truebluecuisine.com · website: www.truebluecuisine.com

zambuca italian restaurant + bar

On the third floor of Pan Pacific Singapore Hotel, Zambuca Italian Restaurant & Bar is yet another fine-dining beauty from the Michelangelo Group. Perhaps a more refined alternative to Michelangelo's and Original Sin of Holland Village fame, Zambuca Italian Restaurant & Bar is where you impress your clients or woo your potential wife (or husband). Rich materials, dark ebony wood and teakwood flooring combine with soft lighting to create a distinctive look; the intimate, sophisticated atmosphere is imbued with a certain noir chic that sets the scene for the fantastic fare to come.

Behind the scenes—striving to keep everyone happy—is executive chef, Dennis Sim. He works closely with group director, Angelo Sanelli, to come up with a classic Italian menu jazzed up with modern touches. The result is a great balance between the modern and the traditional, a somewhat avant-garde Italian cuisine. Popular favourites include original seafood and game classics, while the daily chef's specials keep the menu fresh.

Diners may wish to start their meal with the *foie gras* or *cappesante*. The *foie gras* is pan-fried and served on toasted walnut bread, glazed with port wine and vanilla bean, along with poached figs and passion fruit and apricot jam—a balance between sweet and savoury. The *cappesante* is a portion of pan-seared diver scallops slathered with orange hollandaise sauce that is then gratinated and topped with a king crab and cilantro salad.

THIS PAGE (FROM TOP): The restaurant serves classic Italian cuisine in addition to spiced-up modern versions of traditional dishes; complementing the fine fare on offer, the interior is the epitome of elegance and style.

OPPOSITE (FROM TOP): Pick up a cocktail from the bar to help you relax after a long day; the dessert menu includes familiar Italian favourites such as tiramisu, warm chocolate cake and crème brûlée.

...a classic Italian menu jazzed up with modern touches.

seats
80 • bar: 20 • wine cellar: 12

food
Italian

drink
extensive wine list • cocktails

features
wine cellar and private dining room • catering • wine dinners • special events • private and corporate functions

nearby
Central Business District • Marina Bay • Singapore River • Padang • Esplanade–Theatres on the Bay • Suntec Singapore International Convention and Exhibition Centre • Boat Quay • Clarke Quay • Millennia Walk • Robertson Walk • cenotaph

contact
7 Raffles Boulevard,
level 3 Pan Pacific Singapore, Singapore 039595 •
telephone: +65.6337 8086 •
facsimile: +65.6338 1157 •
email: manager@zambuca.com.sg •
website: www.zambuca.com.sg

Pasta specials begin with the *frutti de mare*. A selection of fresh seafood is combined with herbs and white wine, then served with al dente pasta—prepared just the way it should be—in aglio olio or tomato sauce. The duo of ravioli may appeal to those who prefer a variety of tastes in one portion. Squid ink ravioli stuffed with lobster and Alaskan crab mousse is one half of the duo, and saffron ravioli with salmon and trout, the other. The former is accompanied by an exquisite sea urchin cream sauce while the latter is drizzled with smoked capsicum sauce.

For mains, the lemon sole is a pan-fried fillet in lemon butter caper sauce—an ideal combination—presented with pearl vegetables.

In the mood for some red meat? An order of the *manzo alla griglia*—grilled beef tenderloin and a serving of kipler potatoes paired with decadent *foie gras jus* and truffles—may be just what you're looking for. To end a meal, the *crème brûlée* is a must-try. Save the rest of the delicious dessert menu for your return.

The restaurant's crowning glory is its wine cellar. Set in the centre of the establishment, this glass-walled room is lined with racks of wine of all price ranges from all over the world. The cellar can also seat 12 people comfortably, making it the perfect private dining room for an important occasion. In all, if you want to impress someone, but wish to relax while doing so, then Zambuca is your place.

chinatown+arabstreet
+littleindia

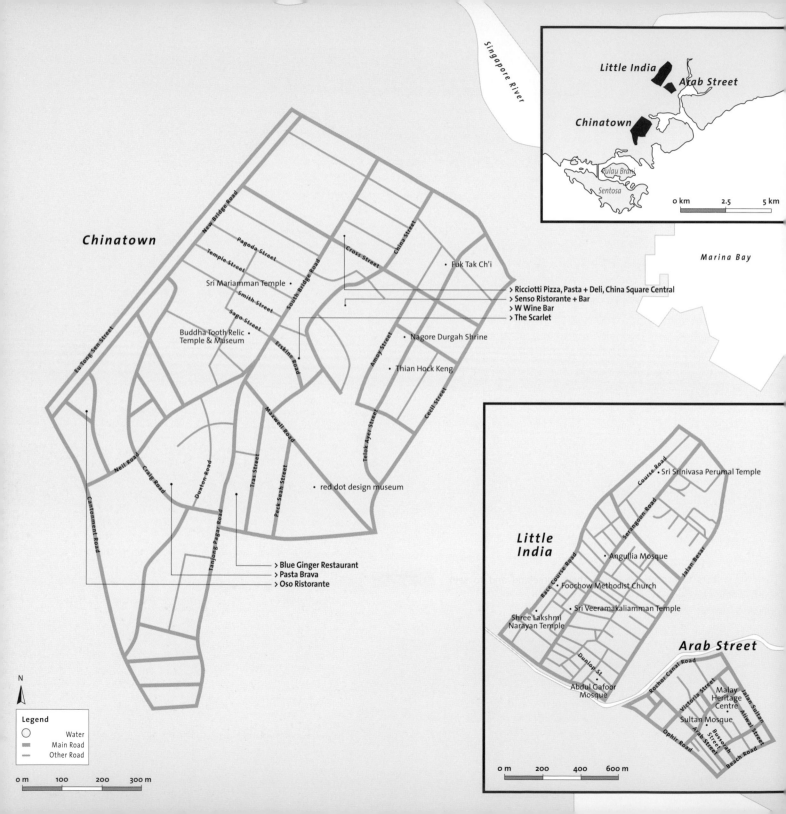

Chinatown

New Bridge Road

Pagoda Street

Temple Street

Sri Mariamman Temple

Smith Street

Sago Street

South Bridge Road

Cross Street

China Street

Erskine Road

Buddha Tooth Relic
Temple & Museum

Eu Tong Sen Street

Maxwell Road

Neil Road

Craig Road

Duxton Road

Cantonment Road

Tanjong Pagar Road

Tras Street

Peck Seah Street

• Fuk Tak Ch'i

> Ricciotti Pizza, Pasta + Deli, China Square Central
> Senso Ristorante + Bar
> W Wine Bar
> The Scarlet

Amoy Street

• Nagore Durgah Shrine

• Thian Hock Keng

Telok Ayer Street

Cecil Street

• red dot design museum

> Blue Ginger Restaurant
> Pasta Brava
> Oso Ristorante

Singapore River

Little India

Arab Street

Chinatown

Pulau Brani

Sentosa

0 km   2.5   5 km

Marina Bay

Little India

Course Road

• Sri Srinivasa Perumal Temple

Serangoon Road

Race Course Road

Jalan Besar

• Angullia Mosque

• Foochow Methodist Church

• Sri Veeramakaliamman Temple

Shree Lakshmi
Narayan Temple

Dunlap St.

Abdul Gafoor
Mosque

Arab Street

Rochar Canal Road

Victoria Street

Malay
Heritage
Centre

Jalan Sultan

Aliwal Street

Sultan Mosque

Bussorah Street

Arab Street

Ophir Road

Beach Road

0 m   200   400   600 m

N

Legend

○ Water
— Main Road
— Other Road

0 m   100   200   300 m

chinatown + arab street + little india

Apart from the religious and cultural landmarks that dot its cityscape, Singapore has little enclaves that are specific to different ethnic groups—Chinatown, Arab Street and Little India. These areas were created as a result of the administrative policies implemented by the British during their 144 years of colonial rule. To ensure better handling of complex ethnic affairs, the British split the island into parts, and had different racial groups settle in different areas. Arab and Muslim immigrants from the Malay Archipelago settled in the Kampong Glam area, where they built the imposing Sultan Mosque in 1928. The various Chinese communities congregated in the bustling streets of the area that came to be known as Chinatown. The Indians, mostly from south India, settled along the Serangoon and Rochor areas, known today as Little India.

Although the racial segregation in Singapore is now a thing of the past, the different areas continue to retain their distinct characteristics—passed on by the people who lived there. Chinatown's shophouses and buildings radiate old-world charm within its streets, while Arab Street's carpet traders and rattan shops carry on their traditional vocations alongside quaint bars and boutiques, and a host of Arab, Egyptian, Turkish and Lebanese restaurants. Little India continues to be the focal point of the Indian community, with a mix of temples and mosques, grocers who stock foodstuff and spices not found elsewhere, and boutiques that bring in the latest fashion trends from the Indian subcontinent.

These ethnic quarters, once a favourite of artists, have mushroomed into alternative enclaves—think showrooms of up-and-coming local designers and cutting-edge art galleries—with culture bursting at the seams.

PAGE 102: Lanterns like these are often used to give the streets of Chinatown a more festive air during major festivals.

THIS PAGE: An intricately crafted paper lantern is hoisted for a performance during the Hungry Ghost Festival.

chinatown

Chinese immigrants arrived from various parts of China in large numbers to escape poverty in their homeland and to seek economic opportunities. They set sail for promised lands 'south of the ocean', having heard stories about the gold and riches in those countries, and landed in places we know today as Singapore, Malaysia and Indonesia. Chinatown, although referred to in the singular, was a place where immigrants from different parts of China lived and worked. Eventually, they created distinct pockets of culture and cuisine within this stretch—modelled on the towns and villages that the immigrants had left behind.

One of the main sub-districts in Chinatown is Kreta Ayer, meaning 'water cart' in Malay. The name was derived from the bullock carts that once carried water to Chinatown from nearby wells. Chinatown's main thoroughfares are the pedestrian streets of Trengganu, Banda, Pagoda, Sago, Smith and Mosque streets. Adjacent areas like Keong Saik Road, Club Street and Ann Siang Hill for the most part form the outer periphery of Chinatown, but they take on a markedly different feel from the interior, and are home to some of the most exciting shops and restaurants on the island.

arab street

Kampong Glam, formerly home to Malay and Arab communities, was a bustling hub for carpet and textile traders. While a number of shops dealing in these businesses can still be found here, it's hard to believe that as recently as a few years ago Arab Street sported little else other than shops selling fabrics and carpets. These days Arab Street presents a very different, inviting façade.

A mix of good Middle Eastern restaurants, quaint bars and designer boutiques draws young hipsters who are keen to soak up the bohemian atmosphere, infused with a bit of flavoured *shisha* smoke. With almost all restaurants in the area providing alfresco seats to recline on, visitors can laze the evening away while sampling the cuisines from Arabia, Turkey, Egypt and Lebanon, with pulsating Egyptian music in the background. The handful of boutiques and bars that have sprung up around Haji Lane make the neighbourhood a laid-back alternative to the sophisticated venues concentrated in and around the Orchard Road and Civic District areas.

little india

The focal point of the Indian community, Little India has held on stubbornly to its cultural roots. Although largely South Indian in character, reflecting the heritage of the majority of Singapore's local Indian population, it is marked by diversity in culture, food, language and religion.

Little India will surprise you at every corner—for instance, you can have your fortune told by a parrot from the street astrologers along the shophouses near Tekka Centre, Upper Dickson Road and Dunlop Street. The parrot is kept in a cage and when called, it will come out, flip through a pile of fortune cards and pick one out for you. If you are prefer a more human touch, make bookings with one of the many palmists or astrologers within the area.

Follow the scent of spices to the last spice grinding outfit in Singapore on Cuff Road, and join others to get a custom blend of spices; have a *henna* tattoo done with Indian or Arabic designs; dabble in *ayurveda* or herbal products; and taste a *paan*—betel nut enhanced with special flavours and wrapped in betel leaves—from the *paan* seller near Little India Arcade.

THIS PAGE (FROM TOP): Purchase a paper umbrella or two in Chinatown as souvenirs; uncover your future—get a parrot in Little India to pick a fortune card specially for you.
OPPOSITE: A man reads the Koran inside the Sultan Mosque.

...diversity in culture, food, language and religion.

sights + sounds

chinatown

Chinatown's shophouses and temples, nestled amidst modern shopping centres and buildings, impart a sense of nostalgic charm.

Start your tour near Pagoda Street, where the opium dens of yore have been replaced by tailors, and camera and trinket stores. Then make a beeline for the **Chinatown Heritage Centre** (48 Pagoda Street) to get a sense of the history behind these streets. The lives of immigrants who once lived in these quarters are presented in compelling exhibits—audio and visual pieces that feature typical scenes from Chinatown at the turn of the last century.

When newcomers first set foot on land after an arduous voyage across the South China Sea, they headed straight for **Thian Hock Keng** (158 Telok Ayer Street), the Temple of Heavenly Bliss, to offer prayers and joss sticks. Established as a place of worship for Mazu, the Taoist goddess of the sea and protector of seamen, the temple was a focal point for the Hokkien community.

A recent addition in the area, the **Buddha Tooth Relic Temple and Museum** (288 South Bridge Road) is a grand five-storey structure, comprising a temple and museum housing rare artefacts. The key feature of the temple—and its namesake—is the Buddha's tooth relic, kept in a gold *stupa*, or dome, on the fourth floor.

Fuk Tak Chi (76 Telok Ayer Street), once a shrine set up by Hakka and Cantonese migrants, is now a street museum with artefacts painstakingly collected from former residents.

Singapore's character as a melting pot of various cultures was evident even in its early years. Chinatown's famous religious sites include the **Jamae Chulia Mosque** (218 South Bridge Road) and the **Sri Mariamman Temple** (244 South Bridge Road), the oldest Hindu temple in the country. The Sri Mariamman Temple is known for its annual *theemithi* or fire-walking festival, when devotees fulfil their vows by walking across a bed of burning coals. The festival is usually held in October.

For a contemporary monument, drop by the **red dot design museum** (28 Maxwell Road). Formerly the premises of the traffic police headquarters, it now houses a design museum with fascinating installations and exhibitions, as well as the premises of top design professionals. Also located here are some lovely cafés.

The Screening Room (12 Ann Siang Hill) combines food, film and nightlife in a five-storey shophouse. Screenings are held every evening at 8 pm, six days a week.

Weave past Smith Street, and head towards the back of Chinatown Complex. Tucked away from view, you will find shops with amazing displays of paper houses, money and cars. These are burnt as part of the Chinese custom of ancestor worship.

arab street

With evocative street names like Haji Lane, Baghdad Street, Muscat Street and Kandahar Street, this area can seem like an entirely different part of town—maybe even a city on its own.

THIS PAGE (CLOCKWISE FROM TOP LEFT): Gods and mythical characters are often painted or carved on the doors of many Chinese temples; the spire of the Sri Mariamman Temple is an integral part of Chinatown's landscape; housed in the former traffic police headquarters, the striking red dot design museum is well-known for its exhibitions and installations.

OPPOSITE: The Buddha Tooth Relic Temple and Museum may not have been in Chinatown for long, but it has already claimed a place as a defining feature of the area.

red dot design museum

Its ambience calls Middle Eastern towns to mind, accentuated by the *azan*, or call to prayer, which emanates from the **Sultan Mosque** (3 Muscat Street) five times every day.

The textile trade, established by early Arab merchants who made the area their home, lives on to this day—colourful bales of fabric and carpets continue to line the streets of the neighbourhood.

Towering over the fashionable boutiques and cafés, several religious monuments stand testament to the area's age-old links to the different Muslim communities.

The elegant **Alsagoff Arab School** (111 Jalan Sultan) is a prominent historical building. Built in 1912 by an influential Arab family, it continues to serve as one of the many schools that impart Islamic education in Singapore. The **Hajjah Fatimah Mosque** (4001 Beach Road), with its distinctive minaret, beautiful stained-glass windows and harmonious blend of European and Islamic architectural styles, is probably the most significant place of worship for Muslims after the Sultan Mosque.

Distinguished by its golden dome and sky-blue tiles, the **Malabar Mosque** (471 Victoria Street) is the spiritual home to the Malabari Muslims of Kerala who, like the Arabs, arrived centuries ago.

little india

Early Indian immigrants in Singapore settled around Little India after they were forced to move from Chulia Kampung—their earlier location—due to overcrowding. The enclave's location near the Serangoon River made it suitable for the raising of cattle and other livestock. The sight of cattle pens around the vicinity gave rise to the nickname of *kandang kerbau* (Malay for 'buffalo pen').

Over the years, Little India has become a focal point for the South Asian community in Singapore. Home to a variety of shops that offer products ranging from clothes to flower garlands and gold, Little India's bustling landscape reflects the subcontinent's diversity of cultures.

A dominant feature of Little India's landscape is the plethora of religious centres—the horizon is marked by the spires of Hindu temples, the minarets of mosques and the towers of churches. Built by migrants who wished to preserve their way of life, these landmarks are a synthesis of culture and style. The dominant feature of south Indian temples is the *gopuram*, or temple towers, with intricately carved scenes from the pantheon of legends.

Held at the beginning of the year, the Thaipusam festival brings hundreds of Hindu devotees, who walk through the streets of Little India carrying milk-pots or elaborate metal structures called *kavadis*. Some devotees also pierce skewers through their bodies as part of the ritual.

Witness small and large ceremonies at the **Sri Srinivasa Perumal Temple** (397 Serangoon Road) and **Sri Veeramakaliamman Temple** (141 Serangoon Road), built in honour of Hindu deities Vishnu and Kali respectively. The **Shree Lakshmi Narayan Temple** (5 Chander Road) is an example of the north Indian style of architecture and worship.

Members from non-Hindu communities have also made their home in this area. The **Kampong Kapor Methodist Church** (3 Kampong Kapor Road), built over 100 years ago, and the **Central Sikh Temple** (2 Towner Road) are important places of worship for the Christians and the Sikhs respectively.

The elegant **Abdul Gafoor Mosque** (41 Dunlop Street) serves the south Indian Muslim community. Built in the early 1990s, the mosque's Moorish arches and calligraphic inscriptions make it one of the most stunning mosques in Singapore.

THIS PAGE (CLOCKWISE FROM TOP RIGHT): An artist tries to capture the beauty of the Sultan Mosque in a sketch; devotees with piercings like these walk several kilometres to fulfil their vows at Thaipusam; Thaipusam is celebrated elaborately every year with processions led by devotees carrying kavadis.
OPPOSITE: Little boys getting ready to go home after their religious classes at the Abdul Gafoor Mosque.

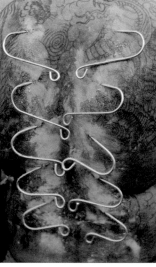

restaurants + bars + cafés

chinatown

As expected, Chinese food of all varieties is to be found here. The **Majestic Restaurant** (New Majestic Hotel, 31–37 Bukit Pasoh Road) is the first stop for modern Chinese. Chef Yong's award-winning Cantonese cuisine paired with fine wines ensures the best culinary experience in this part of the city. The interiors of **Taste Paradise** (48–49 Mosque Street) are the first hints of their well-executed modern Chinese fusion. Its signature carrot cake, curry-mayo prawns, crispy spare ribs and pan-seared *foie gras* with prawns are well-known favourites.

To get a better understanding of the variations in Chinese cuisine, sample the regional Chinese dishes. **Beng Hiang Restaurant**'s (112–116 Amoy Street) Hokkien cuisine offers specialities like oyster omelette, *hokkien mee* and roast chicken. **Lee Kui Restaurant** (8 Mosque Street) specialises in Teochew cuisine and is particularly well known for delicacies such as cold crabs, braised goose and yam paste. Homesick Szechuanese students and expatriates flock to **Hometown Restaurant** (9 Smith Street) for its spicy offerings. The house speciality, which translates as 'saliva chicken', was perhaps named for the salivating effects it brings on.

An unbeatable culinary experience can be found at **Red Star Restaurant** (Block 54 Chin Swee Road), an old-fashioned *dim sum* restaurant, considered an institution in Chinatown. Red Star has such a high feel-good, nostalgic quotient that Chinese TV celebrities are often seen here having their breakfast.

A household name in traditional Chinese pastries, **Tong Heng** (285 South Bridge Road) has been producing barbecued pork crispy pastries and egg tarts since 1920. **Mei Heong Yuen Dessert** (65–67 Temple Street), an old-style shop in the midst of Chinatown's bustle, has a tempting array of traditional desserts such as Chinese almond cream, sesame and peanut pastes, mango *sago*, and Chinese pastries such as steamed yam cakes and water chestnut cakes. For a good cup of *kopi*—or local coffee—and toast with *kaya* (coconut jam), look for **Tong Ya Coffeeshop** (36 Keong Saik Road).

Indulge in a wide range of local favourites from the alfresco food stalls of **Chinatown Food Street**, which recreate the food carts of the past in a contemporary setting.

Chinatown also hosts other types of cuisine. **Gorkha Grill** (21 Smith Street) serves Nepali dishes such as *momo*, chilli chicken and papaya prawns. Daily specials at the **Tiffin Club** (16 Jiak Chuan Road), based on Adrian Zecha's secret family recipes, are a good way to sample Eurasian food. Steak-lovers in the city prize the cuts at **Les Bouchons** (7 Ann Siang Road), a Parisian steak frites bistro that serves excellent beef and hand-cut fries, in a cosy setting.

Restaurant Ember (Hotel 1929, 50 Keong Saik Road) offers modern European fare, while **Nicolas Le Restaurant** (35 Keong Saik Road) is Nicolas Joanny's acclaimed French fine-dining establishment. **Oso Ristorante**'s (46 Bukit Pasoh Road) elegant northern Italian dishes have won many fans, while the homemade

pasta and homey ambience at the cosy **Pasta Brava** (11 Craig Road) have delighted pasta-lovers for more than 10 years.

Goto (14 Ann Siang Road) is an exclusive, reservations-only operation with exquisite *kaiseki* options—expect to be overwhelmed by *kaiseiki* master Goto Hisao's sheer skill. Every Sunday, Goto hands over its space to **enso kitchen** (14 Ann Siang Hill). Here, chef Danny Chu pays homage to the philosophy of *shojin ryori*. Trained in the kitchens of Kyoto's shrines, Chu brings out the nuances of natural ingredients in this vegetarian culinary genre, which originated in the Zen temples of Japan.

Some of Singapore's best bars are to be found in this area. **Magma** (2 Bukit Pasoh Road), a German wine bistro and deli, features wines from 13 wine-producing regions in Germany, pork knuckles, sausages, *flammkuchen*, takeaway deli treats, as well as German cooking classes. **Beaujolais Wine Bar** (1 Ann Siang Hill) is a tiny wine bar housed in a cosy shophouse; while **Le Carillon de L'Angelus** (24 Ann Siang Road) is perfect for after-work drinks.

Baretto (46 Bukit Pasoh Road), the intimate wine bar attached to Oso Ristorante, turns the spotlight on the careful selection of Italian wines in its massive cellar. The Majestic Hotel is well known for its avant-garde **Majestic Bar** (41 Bukit Pasoh Road), which is part chic watering hole, part installation art.

With a choice of movies, drinks and a fantastic view—all in one place—**The Screening Room**'s (12 Ann Siang Hill) rooftop bar and basement

THIS PAGE (FROM TOP): Savour a serving of pan-fried rib-eye fillet in homemade sesame sauce, garnished with kimchi, at the Majestic Restaurant; steamed shrimp dumplings are a key component in dim sum; sample vegetarian delights cooked in a unique style at enso kitchen.

OPPOSITE: The tastefully appointed interiors of the Majestic Restaurant are the perfect setting for a meal.

restaurants + bars + cafés

THIS PAGE (ANTICLOCKWISE FROM TOP): Enjoy a drink, and the scenic view, at the Screening Room's rooftop terrace; there is no dearth of good places to appreciate a glass of wine; plush seats at the Scarlet Hotel's Bold bar add to the cosy ambience.

OPPOSITE (CLOCKWISE FROM TOP LEFT): Peppermint tea, served in ornamental Arabic glasses; shisha or hookahs are used to smoke flavoured tobacco; tourists and locals alike lap up the Middle Eastern atmosphere and cuisine in Arab Street; kebabs with Arabic bread, a favoured combination in the area.

whiskey bar are lush venues to kick back and relax. The Scarlet has two commendable options—**Breeze** offers panoramic views of Chinatown and the financial district from the rooftop, while the opulent hotel's lobby bar, **Bold** tempts with premium vodkas and an array of finger food and desserts.

arab street

Arab Street's cafés are run by expatriates from various Middle Eastern countries whose cuisines they profess to serve. A fine spread of favourites from across the Arab world and Turkey offers diners a whirlwind tour of the region's cuisine.

Indulge in Yemeni lamb stew, *babaganoush*, freshly baked breads with dips, and wash it down with a refreshing *karkadeh* hibiscus fizz drink. The restaurants remain true to their cultural roots—alcohol is not served in many venues in this area.

Look out for **Café Le Caire** (39 Arab Street), the one that started it all. Owner Ameen Ali Talib, a former academic, set out to revive Arab culture in Singapore back in 2001. Today, the line of Arab restaurants down the stretch owe their presence in part to his influence.

Al Tazzag Egyptian Restaurant (24 Haji Lane), a small Egyptian restaurant in a cozy nook of Haji Lane, has won many fans for its kebabs. **Alaturka** (16 Bussorah Street) has been the stalwart of Turkish food for years, but there are now more choices such as **Sufi** (43 Arab Street), which offers laid-back comfort and commendable food. For those craving Moroccan specialities, there are some exquisite options here, including **Mosi Café** (32 Haji Lane) and **Deli Moroccan** (30 Bussorah Street). **El Sheikh** (18 Pahang Street), set a little further away, boasts excellent Lebanese fare.

To sample local Malay cuisine in style, step into **Restoran Tepak Sireh** (73 Sultan Gate), a respected Malay restaurant nestled in a historic building that once housed royalty.

Indulge in popular Singaporean favourites like *roti prata*, *murtabak* and *biryani* from the many stalls that dot the sidewalks. A good *prata* and *murtabak* is best paired with a frothy cup of *teh tarik*—a combination close to many Singaporeans' hearts.

The **Rich & Good Cake Shop** (24 Kandahar Street) lives up to its name with its much-loved swiss rolls. The durian roll is critically acclaimed, while for those with tamer tastebuds, the cream cheese carrot cake and *kaya* rolls might be a better choice.

The Japanese chocolate boutique **Blue Ribbon** (42 Kandahar Street) is relatively new, but is well-known among the city's knowledgeable foodies. Blue Ribbon specialises in pure handmade Japanese chocolates, not available anywhere else in Southeast Asia. Straight from Hokkaido chocolatiers, the delicious white chocolates are made with Hokkaido's fresh milk, and are worth their weight in gold.

Look out for the discreet **B Bakery** (15 Bussorah Street). The bakery has wonderful passion fruit cheesecakes, strawberry shortcakes, sticky buns and other desserts, as well as sandwiches for those who prefer something less sweet.

THIS PAGE (CLOCKWISE FROM TOP LEFT): A classic Indian meal usually consists of breads and assorted side-dishes made from lentils and vegetables; cooked with a blend of spices, mutton masala is a perenniel favourite among Indian-food lovers; fish cooked in curry, lamb stew and steamed basmati rice are favoured elements in Indian cuisine.
OPPOSITE: Indulge in khulfi, a homemade ice-cream-like dessert, in a classy setting at the Khulfi Bar.

Keeping in line with cultural norms, there are few pubs and bars in this area. However, the options that do exist are worth a visit, or two. Prominent names here include **Going Om** (63 Haji Lane) and **Blu Jaz** (11 Bali Lane). Going Om, run by two friendly young men, combines food, drink and fun with new-age subculture and activities in an intimate, comfortable space. Blu Jaz is the bar heavyweight in the area, packing in the crowds every night with live music, a long list of drinks, good food and its eclectic décor.

little india

Settle in for lunch at home-grown **Komala Vilas Restaurant** (76 Serangoon Road). The restaurant still maintains its old-school charm, and serves traditional south Indian meals on a banana leaf. For the best in Singaporean Indian cuisine, head down to the **Gayatri Restaurant** (122 Race Course Lane) or **Sakunthala's Food Palace** (66 Race Course Road).

A famous name in the food scene, **Muthu's Curry** (138 Race Course Road) has won several accolades—mostly for its fish-head curry, and some for its décor, which was revamped with a lavish makeover a few years ago. Tuck into a variety of chicken, mutton and seafood dishes at **Banana Leaf Apollo** (54/56/58 Race Course Road). As the name indicates, the food is served on a banana leaf, with rice and curry being the staple for every meal.

For a different experience, try having lunch at **Iniavan's Indian Cuisine** (37 Chander Road). Make your selection from dozens of options, each represented by coloured toothpicks. Hand over the toothpicks to the staff, who will bring the dishes to your table along with rice and vegetables.

Regional specialities from India are also to be found here. Have a meal at **Swaadhisht** (47 Chander Road) for a taste of the cuisine from the southern, coastal state of Kerala. Or sample dishes cooked with a special blend of spices, native to a south Indian town called Chettinad, at **Anjappar Authentic Chettinaad Restaurant** (76–78 Race Course Road).

Lagnaa (6 Upper Dickson Road), a quaint restaurant on the upper floors of a shophouse, has taken comfort to a new level. Relax on cushions while you tuck in to 'fondue curry', a house speciality. For the perfect dessert, walk into **Khulfi Bar** (15 Upper Dickson Road) across the street and sample *khulfi* or homemade Indian ice cream in a variety of flavours. Khulfi Bar also has an array of Indian souvenirs that make for good collectibles or gifts.

For a wide variety of *naans* or Indian breads, *tandoori* dishes and curries, head towards **Jade of India** (172 Race Course Road), or try north Indian and Nepali dishes at **Shish Mahal** (Albert Court Hotel). One of the best-known restaurants in the area, **Nirvana** (Fortuna Hotel, 2 Owen Road) boasts a whopping 146 items on its menu, including many traditional favourites.

The areas bordering Jalan Besar are home to some of the best names in Chinese food, with **Pu Tien** (127 Kitchener Road) among those receiving favourable reviews.

Established by migrants from the coastal city of Pu Tien, signature dishes like razor clams and homemade beancurd are especially popular among patrons. Run by a Chinese couple who lived in Thailand, **Northern Thai** (1 Tyrwhitt Road) is known for its *tomyam* soup, served with fried fish slices and tasty pineapple rice. **Hillman** (135 Kitchener Road), famous since the 1960s for its old-school cuisine, is popular for its claypot specialities and paper-wrapped chicken.

Given the strong leanings towards vegetarianism in Indian culture, those looking for alternatives to meat have plenty of choice in Little India. Beyond the Indian restaurants, which offer a variety of vegetarian options, there is also **Food #03** (109 Rowell Road). Its contemporary cuisine includes freshly baked breads, good pizzas and an innovative *tempeh* (Indonesian soybean cake) burger. **7 Sensations** (16 Madras Street) delights with regional and international dishes such as *gado gado*, *moussaka* and pumpkin salad.

An influx of cafés and pubs has livened up the area in recent years. **Stiff Chilli** (279 Jalan Besar) offers laid-back Aussie-Bali charm, excellent gelato and pizzas, as well as take-home packs of coffee and tea that make worthy gifts.

Spend a relaxed evening at the **Prince of Wales** (101 Dunlop Street), a pub with live music most nights and a selection of cold beer. Indulge in *tapas* and nibbles at **Zsofi Tapas Bar** (68 Dunlop Street) or sample French-style duck confit at **The Black Sheep Café** (35 Mayo Street).

shopping

chinatown

Chinatown offers some of the best deals for those who wish to take home something a little different.

If you are interested in natural herbs and medicines, step into **Eu Yan Sang** (269 South Bridge Road), an established name in traditional medicine. For the best in *bak kwa*—barbecued pork slices that are a favoured gift during Chinese festive seasons—**Bee Cheng Hiang** (189 New Bridge Road) and **Lim Chee Guan** (203 New Bridge Road) are the main brands to look for.

Attend a tea appreciation workshop at **Tea Chapter** (9A/11 Neil Road) and learn how to brew Chinese tea the traditional way. The well-stocked shop also sells a large variety of tea leaves and beautiful tea sets.

For a different experience, drop by **red dot design museum**'s (28 Maxwell Road) MAAD weekend market, held every first Saturday and Sunday of the month. Best described as a carefully curated garage sale, it's the ideal place to pick up original works by artists and designers. Performances and live street art liven up the experience.

Fans of older, classic camera models such as Rolleis, Seagulls and Voigtlanders can find them at **Fotografix Marketing** (133 New Bridge Road).

A space devoted entirely to literature for the discerning, **BooksActually** (5 Ann Siang Hill) offers an impressive selection of books, retro oddities, beautiful notebooks and stationery, as well as a selection of Holga, Lomography, Agfa, Polaroid cameras and spy cameras.

25 degree Celsius (25 Keong Saik Road), a cookbook store, boasts a massive collection of cookbooks and food-related publications. The test kitchen offers a selection of dishes straight out of their cookbooks and serves them in the attached café. Look out for **Sia Huat** (7, 9 and 11 Temple Street), a wholesale emporium of kitchen products, tableware, utensils and even kitchen uniforms. Stocking a wide variety of kitchen products, including leading brands for consumer and industrial use, it is a good place for professional cooks and culinary enthusiasts.

The boutiques at Club Street and Ann Siang Hill offer a varied collection of clothes, accessories and décor items, sourced from local as well as international designers.

Venue (44–46 Club Street) is the leading retailer in sports couture and high-end street fashion. In addition to Alexander McQueen and Mihara Yasuhiro's Puma collections, up-and-coming labels like Bikkembergs, Guilty Brotherhood and Raf Simons also have a strong presence.

Cayen (54A Club Street) offers ready-to-wear and custom-made clothing. Complement them with shoes from **Eve** (21 Club Street), which offers collections by designers like Rupert Sanderson and Hetty Rose.

Nearby, Ann Siang Road is home to **STYLE:NORDIC** (39 Ann Siang Road), specialising in Scandinavian fashion such as Nudie Jeans and Filippa K, along with furniture and timepieces from brands like Hag and Skagen. **Asylum** (22 Ann Siang Road) is an experimental concept store with limited edition sneakers, quirky gifts,

indie music, and edgy fashion from Grace Tan's critically acclaimed Kwodrent collection.

Keeping with the theme of progressive cult fashion, **Front Row**'s (5 Ann Siang Road) collection from A. P. C., Woods & Woods, Kitsune and more will keep the cool-hunters busy, with pop art exhibitions that add oomph to the interior décor.

Strangelets (87 Amoy Street) is a curious nook full of crafts from Imiso, Nils Holger Moorman, Astier de Villatte and other heroes of contemporary design.

arab street

There is no antique shop quite like **Grandfather's Collection** (42 Bussorah Street), which has a collection of nostalgic knick knacks that will take you back to various stages of Singapore history. Out in the garden, enjoy a cup of freshly made coffee from the 1960s coffeeshop setup. The assembled 'set pieces' may seem like museum exhibits, and indeed they are. For more curios and collectibles from the Soviet era, such as watches and cameras, step into the **Dinky Di Store** (Golden Landmark Hotel, 390 Victoria Street).

To pick up a unique perfume redolent with the fragrance of Arabia, walk over to **Jamal Kazura Aromatics** (21 Bussorah Street), an all-natural custom perfumery and boutique. Choose Arabic and Egyptian scents, oils, creams and soaps, or have the in-store fragrance wizards concoct a personalised perfume with five types of oils. Ready-made or specially mixed, the ornate vials they come in are bound to be a hit.

THIS PAGE (CLOCKWISE FROM TOP): BooksActually boasts a collection of literature, beautiful stationery and vintage collectibles; trinkets like these bells can be brought from one of the many shops that dot Chinatown's streets; sign up for a course and learn the nuances of the art of brewing tea.
OPPOSITE: Chinatown's bustling streets come to life at night when more people frequent the street stalls.

shopping

For those who wish to pick up souvenirs for the home or gifts, Arab Street and its environs are ideal. Weave in and out of the shops and purchase crystalware or crafts made from cane and rattan.

The textile and carpet shops of Arab Street offer a wide selection of gifts. **Poppy Fabric** (111 Arab Street) deals in exquisite silks from all over the world, while **Basharahil Bros** (101 Arab Street) boasts a gorgeous range of batik, silk and chiffon. Seek out **Silkland** (49 Arab Street), wholesaler of fine silks from India. This second-floor showroom may be a bit hard to locate (hint: entrance is at 20 Haji Lane), but the Indian silks and linens are well worth the effort.

The area's fashion centres are concentrated on Haji Lane, a bohemian street that proudly runs counter to mainstream sophistication. The **House of Japan** (55 Haji Lane) may look deceptively normal from the outside, but step in and find yourself surrounded by branded vintage clothes imported from Japan. Sister-shop **Jap Vintage** (78 Haji Lane) has a beautiful range of hand-sewn traditional Japanese wear, including kimonos.

Victoria JoMo (9 Haji Lane) gives the vintage theme an update, with trendy new items juxtaposed against a classic retro décor.

Know It Nothing (51 Haji Lane) offers art-fashion label-wear and sports couture footwear. Expect brands like Wood & Wood, Ctrl Clothing, Umbro by Kim Jones, P. A. M. and others. **Soon Lee** (56 Haji Lane) is the address to hit for shoes, bags, clothes and accessories.

Billet Doux's (45A Arab Street, entrance via 16A Haji Lane) homemade accessories complement the designer line-up, which include Svensson Jeans, Common Projects and Alex & Chloe. The **White Room** (37 Haji Lane) offers local labels Fantastik Antik and Fru Fru & Tigerlily alongside edgy global brands.

The black-and-white **Salad** (25/27 Haji Lane) serves up a hearty bowl of bags, shoes, jewellery and oddities including the occasional piece of furniture. Run by passionate owners, the word 'exclusive' is taken rather seriously here—the availability of most items in the store is restricted to just six pieces.

The quirky wallpaper, vintage fabrics, bags and homeware at **Pluck** (31/33 Haji Lane) are some of the best in home décor, and the in-store ice cream parlour which stocks locally made gourmet ice cream is yet another reason to drop by.

little india

Shop for the latest in Indian fashion from *saris* to *salwar kameez* and *kurtas* at **Stylemart** (149 Selegie Road). Not sure what is the best choice? Friendly assistants will help you pick and choose.

For a selection of modern Indian clothes with classic cuts and made of quality fabric, drop by at **Sheetal** (136/136A Serangoon Road) and **Jinder's** (153A Selegie Road). They offer Indian attire, with appropriate styles to suit different personalities. Get a ready-made outfit or get one tailored. Either way, you will walk away with an exclusive one-of-a-kind piece. To complete your outfit, pick up bangles and earrings from **Amba Ji International** (171 Selegie Road). Bring along your outfit and the shop's assistants will coordinate the preferred accessories to a T.

Be dazzled by the gold on display in the line of jewellery shops here. The yellow metal has long been held in high esteem by Indians. Sales skyrocket during festivals like Deepavali and during months marked as especially auspicious for weddings. Purchase exquisitely crafted pieces, or ask resident jewellers to suggest precious stones that will suit you, based on your birth date.

No journey to Little India is complete without venturing into **Mustafa** (145 Syed Alwi Road). The mammoth 6,968-sq m (75,000-sq ft) retailer is open around the clock, with a reputation for selling just about anything. Available within are food, jewellery, clothes, home décor, books, electronics and sports items. With resident foreign exchange services and a café, Mustafa is a place where little can get in the way of a good splurge .

For a different kind of shopping experience, try the **Sungei Road Thieves' Market**. The market historically carried contraband and stolen goods, which explains its name. Now, it retains the same open-air junk market concept, just with vintage items instead of misbegotten gains. On sale are old photographs, amulets, bags, records and laser discs, outdated books and magazines, and even the occasional classic camera. The vendors stay till after sunset, but visit in the early part of the day to get the best bargains.

THIS PAGE (FROM TOP): Complement your outfit with suitable accessories; a plethora of choice in intricately worked gold ornaments awaits at jewellery shops in Little India; silk saris, embroidered with gold brocade, are always fashionable.

OPPOSITE (CLOCKWISE FROM TOP LEFT): Take home Middle Eastern-style souvenirs from Arab Street; batik is a popular fabric choice; select from the assortment of simple or elaborate shawls on offer.

PAGE 122: Dragon motifs are often embroidered on clothing, as these creatures are considered auspicious.

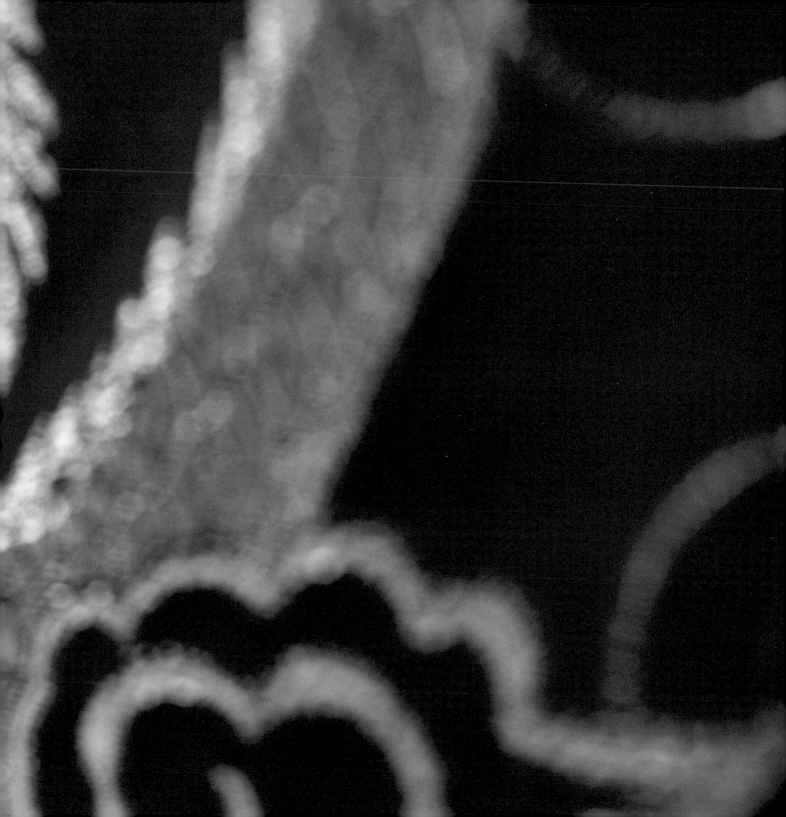

w wine bar

THIS PAGE: *Kick back after a long, tiring day at work and relax with friends over a bottle of fine wine at W Wine Bar.*

OPPOSITE (FROM LEFT): *The well-stocked bar serves virtually any alcoholic drink a guest could want, from fruity cocktails to smooth cognac; both alcoholic and non-alcoholic drinks are available here, and guests can enjoy their choices while lounging in air-conditioned comfort.*

W Wine Bar, located along Club Street, is an interesting addition to the stretch of historical shophouses that have been transformed into trendy lifestyle shops, fine dining restaurants and bars.

The bar occupies the ground level of a shophouse, with a glass façade that blurs the boundary between its interior and exterior spaces. The glass doors can slide back completely to let in fresh air and the vibe of the energetic Club Street. People-watchers will be delighted to find that this also gives a great view for their favourite hobby.

Ambient lights illuminate the interior, which is a blend of pale stone, clear glass and dark wood. Maroon- and pebble-coloured velvet couches are carefully arranged to create comfortable, intimate spaces for quiet business meetings. The plush seating and convivial atmosphere also make it an ideal venue for informal drinks and get-togethers; soothing lounge music is set at a volume that does not drown out conversations.

Over 200 vintage and non-vintage wines are stored in W Wine Bar's temperature-controlled walk-in cellar. Guests are welcome to take a closer look at the labels available. There are Australian wines such as Cloudy Bay, Cape Mentelle and Yalumba; French wines such as Chateau Cheval Blanc, Louis Latour and Dujac; and sweet wines such as Chateau D'Yquem. Moet & Chandon and Krug lead the bar's list of champagnes.

Beverages apart from wine are also served here. Guests have at their fingertips an array of cocktails, cognac, sherry, reserve whiskies and even Scotland's best single malt whisky, The Macallan. Those who want to have some light snacks to accompany their drinks can choose from the menu of finger food. Cigar lovers are not neglected—a range of decadent Havana cigars such as Cohiba, Montecristo and Partagas can be purchased at the bar.

Every month, W Wine Bar organises regular wine-tasting events for its regulars and other wine aficionados. During these sessions, the in-house sommelier shares his knowledge with the guests.

W Wine Bar is affiliated with Senso Ristorante & Bar next door. No two food and beverage establishments could complement each other more perfectly. Guests can loosen up after a long day with a pre-dinner bottle of wine at W Wine Bar, then head to Senso Ristorante & Bar for their meal, bringing their drinks over to accompany the fine cuisine.

Guests may be interested to know that W Wine Bar is available for corporate functions, intimate wine-tasting events and parties. It also offers customised packages.

seats
30

food
finger food

drink
over 200 vintage and non-vintage labels •
full-service bar

features
walk-in wine cellar

nearby
Chinatown • Tanjong Pagar • Ann Siang Hill

contact
11 Club Street, Singapore 069405 •
telephone: +65.6223 3886 •
facsimile: +65.6223 5233 •
email: gina@senso.com.sg •
website: www.wwinebar.sg

the scarlet

THIS PAGE (FROM LEFT): *The elegant lobby, with its gleaming medley of red, black and cream, welcomes visitors; Desire, the hotel's restaurant, offers guests a chance to savour delicious fare in style.*

OPPOSITE (FROM LEFT): *The romantic Passion Suite is ideal for couples and honeymooners; the hotel's impressive façade displays its blend of traditional style and modernity.*

Opened in December 2004 after a thorough and very expensive refurbishment, The Scarlet is an 80-room establishment that combines traditional shophouse architecture with stylish contemporary design. It departs from the predictable mould of city hotels with its five themed suites whose names match the moods their interiors evoke.

Splendour, Passion, Opulent, Lavish and Swank each have different colour schemes, furnishings and amenities that vary according to each room's theme. The Passion Suite, for example, was designed with honeymooners in mind. Its seductive interior, swathed in burgundy, fuchsia, silver and black, makes use of a low ceiling to create an air of intimacy. It also offers its inhabitants a four-poster bed as well as an outdoor jacuzzi.

All of the hotel's 14 premium, 25 executive, 28 deluxe and 8 standard rooms are tailored to the needs of the large numbers of business travellers who come to Singapore. These guestrooms are fully equipped with facilities for guests who are working while on the road. On the other hand, tourists and travellers who are here for leisure will surely appreciate the indulgent comfort offered by these luxurious accommodations after they return from an enjoyable but tiring day of exploring the city-state, sightseeing and shopping.

All rooms at The Scarlet, regardless of type, are decked out with a range of modern amenities. Each room comes with individually controlled air-conditioning, televisions with access to cable channels and complimentary movie channels, desks with data ports for computer and fax connections, personalised wake-up call systems, voicemail message systems, personal bars, electronic door locks and digital in-room safes.

The Scarlet adds a special touch with its choice breakfast sets, a gourmet selection in the personal bar, and evening cocktails, which are served in the privacy of guests' rooms. Guests can choose between goose tempur and non-allergenic foam pillows, and the hotel even has its own brand of bathroom amenities. In addition to DVD players, all rooms also have free unlimited high-speed Internet access. The Sanctum, the hotel's oval-

...combines traditional shophouse architecture with stylish contemporary design.

rooms
5 suites • 14 premium, 25 executive, 28 deluxe and 8 standard rooms

food
Desire: contemporary European • Breeze: alfresco seafood bar and grill

drink
Bold: wine, champagne and cocktails

features
individually-themed suites • outdoor jacuzzi • boutique gift shop • 24-hour in-room dining • voicemail message systems • gym • high-speed Internet access • conference room • laundry service

nearby
Chinatown • Central Business District • dining • bars and clubs • MRT station

contact
33 Erskine Road, Singapore 069333 • telephone: +65.6511 3333 • facsimile: +65.6511 3303 • email: reservations@thescarlethotel.com or enquiry@thescarlethotel.com • website: www.thescarlethotel.com

shaped boardroom, has luxurious furnishings and is equipped with modern conference facilities. The hotel's shop, Flair, boasts gift items sourced from all over the world, many of which are not commonly found in Singapore. For those who have fallen so in love with The Scarlet that they wish to bring home part of the living experience of the hotel, custom-order replicas of room and suite furnishings are available at Flair. The Scarlet's other facilities are likewise packaged as products with distinct identities: Flaunt is the hotel's gym, while Soda is its outdoor jacuzzi.

Desire is the hotel's fine restaurant, which offers a menu of contemporary European cuisine, while Breeze is the alfresco rooftop seafood bar and grill, and Bold is the hotel's lobby bar. In the evenings, a pub crawl could begin at Bold and continue on to the many establishments along vibrant Club Street, which is only a short walk from Erskine Road.

Situated in the city, The Scarlet is a good starting point for guests who want to go sightseeing. Chinatown is just an invigorating 10-minute walk away and the nearest MRT station merely five minutes away on foot.

blue ginger restaurant

THIS PAGE: 'Ngo heong', literally 'five spices' in Cantonese, is a widely known traditional Peranakan dish of seasoned minced meat wrapped in beancurd skin and fried.

OPPOSITE (FROM LEFT): The second floor of the shophouse, like the ground floor, is infused with appealing old-world charm; otak otak is a local favourite.

An ethnic group unique to Southeast Asia, the Peranakans have a rich culinary style that is the result of several centuries of cultural blending and assimilation. Also known as the Straits Chinese and Baba-Nyonya (men being the Babas and women, Nyonyas), their story began with the arrival of Chinese immigrants in the region, many of whom stayed on and intermarried with the local Malay population over several generations. As a result, Peranakan food is heir to flavours not found in any other global cuisine, uniting spice and simplicity, and often featuring tangy, fragrant elements.

Blue ginger is a vital component of the Peranakan taste—the Cantonese call it 'nam kiong' while Malays call it 'galangal'. However, Blue Ginger is also the name of a celebrated Singaporean restaurant that continues to preserve traditional Straits Chinese recipes in a time when they are in danger of being forgotten, while also seeking to bring these distinctive dishes to a wider audience. The Blue Ginger Restaurant is a small but well-loved establishment that does things the old way, inspired by the artistry of grandmothers and memories of sumptuous family meals.

So strong is the Peranakan reverence for food that young women were once judged almost solely on their abilities in the kitchen. Recipes were treated as family heirlooms and passed down from one generation to another in handwritten volumes which were usually fiercely guarded. Peranakan cooking often involves slow and laborious processes—as a result, most meals were prepared at home and enjoyed within the privacy of the home. Add to that the tremendous pride that led most Peranakan cooks to turn their noses up at another's efforts, and the idea of a Peranakan restaurant becomes something of an improbable dream.

Yet the Blue Ginger Restaurant has been wildly succesful, partly due to the fact that modern lifestyles no longer allow for hours spent in a kitchen. Another reason is that the food is so good, it even passes muster with jealous Peranakan grandmothers.

The inside of this modest shophouse is a treasure trove of artefacts and paintings, many telling the story of the island's colonial past. The stage is set for traditional favourites such as *ayam panggang* (de-boned chicken thighs and drumsticks marinated in coconut milk and spices before being grilled), *sambal terong goreng* (deep-fried slivers of eggplant served with fresh chilli paste and sweetened soy sauce) and *otak otak* (soft, spicy cakes of pounded fish enlivened by the addition of turmeric, lime leaves, blue ginger, candlenuts, chilli and shrimp paste).

The restaurant can accommodate up to 70 diners at once over its two floors, but reservations are a good idea. Private dining rooms for a maximum of 40 people are also available, especially useful whenever large Peranakan families need to celebrate without having to keep looking over their shoulders for disapproving neighbours.

seats
70 • private rooms for 12, 20 and 40

food
traditional Peranakan

drink
beverage list

features
period art • Peranakan artefacts •
catering services

nearby
Chinatown • Central Business District •
Tanjong Pagar MRT station

contact
97 Tanjong Pagar Road, Singapore 088518 •
telephone (restaurant): +65.6222 3928 •
telephone (office): +65.6224 4028 •
facsimile: +65.6222 3860 •
email: sue.teo@theblueginger.com •
website: www.theblueginger.com

oso ristorante

THIS PAGE (FROM TOP): *The romantic setting makes Oso Ristorante an ideal choice for celebrating a special occasion; the quaint façade of the new premises at Bukit Pasoh.*

OPPOSITE (FROM TOP): *The capable team of Chef Diego Chiarini and Stephane Colleoni has led the restaurant to success; patrons can sample several varieties of cheese and savour fine Italian and French cuisine.*

It was one of the island country's great paradoxes that despite a sterling reputation for excellence in gastronomy, Singapore always had a bit of a gap to fill when it came to Italian food. While other global cuisines enjoyed strong representation from establishments that soon became local institutions in themselves, it seemed that Italian eateries were known for their short lifespan. They seemed to arrive, and soon say 'arrivederci' ('goodbye').

All that has changed. Since the year 2004, Oso Ristorante has made an inspiring grab for the title of Singapore's best Italian restaurant, exhibiting considerable staying power on the strength of its authentic northern recipes and the talents of head chef Diego Chiarini, who

has worked in the kitchens of Il Carpaccio in Paris and Bice in Tokyo, as well as at the well-regarded local Senso Ristorante & Bar. The spiritedly named Oso ('to dare') rings with the sound of a gauntlet being thrown down.

Along with friend and manager, Stephane Colleoni, Chef Chiarini worked at building the Oso name from a modest shophouse over the past four years—and succeeded wildly. This year, the pair have made an audacious move to a historical three-storey mansion in Bukit Pasoh, expanding the restaurant's scope.

New to the Oso mix are Absinthe, a full-featured French restaurant in its own right, and Baretto, a sleek bar that caters to the restaurants' guests as well as its own select clientele. Acclaimed chef Francois Mermilliod heads the kitchen at Absinthe, while industry veteran Philippe Pau rounds up the new executive team of four as restaurant manager. All three establishments occupy the same beautifully preserved building.

Oso Ristorante now seats 90 at once, with a third of that number comprised of alfresco tables, while Absinthe can accommodate 50. There are also two private dining rooms—Azelia and Billecart Salmon—for parties of up to 26 and 12 respectively. Baretto is licensed to serve 120 patrons, which may prove to be a conservative number given that it boasts the largest selection of French champagnes available locally—around 80 labels.

Staying true to the sophisticated décor of the restaurant's previous incarnation, the new Bukit Pasoh address takes the classic Italian look to greater heights. Located on the second storey, Oso Ristorante receives ample natural light and enjoys scenic views of the quiet tree-shrouded neighbourhood. Careful lighting creates a warm, intimate ambience, which beautifully complements the black feature walls and bold splashes of red fabric.

Fans of the original Oso Ristorante will be relieved to hear that the most important thing about it—the menu—has not been tampered with at all, and popular favourites such as the saffron tagliolini with braised monkfish cheek and the gratinated beef tenderloin with sabayon, potato and white truffle have been retained. The dedicated cheese room has also survived the move, and continues to present a rotating variety of rare and mature cheeses. Experience a delightful interlude here in the cheese room before adjourning to the bar to end a night of exquisite Italian or French dining.

seats
Oso Ristorante: 60 indoor • 30 outdoor • private dining rooms for 26 and 12 • Absinthe: 50 • Baretto: 120

food
Oso Ristorante: Italian • Absinthe: French

drink
Baretto: Italian lounge bar

features
cigar room • cheese room • private dining

nearby
Chinatown • Central Business District • Outram Park MRT station

contact
46 Bukit Pasoh Road, Singapore 089858 • telephone: +65.6327 8378 • facsimile: +65.6224 9610 • email: reservations@oso.sg • website: www.oso.sg

pasta brava

Sometimes eating out feels a little like hard work, and there's nothing you'd like more than a slow-paced, unfussy meal, where you can kick back and fill up on some home cooking. Well, Singapore's Italian answer to that is Pasta Brava. A family-run establishment, this little gem on the outskirts of Chinatown is an institution; the fact that it's been open since 1993 serves to prove the point.

What makes this restaurant so homey is the presence of the warm and gregarious owner, Rolando Luceri. Although he's been in Singapore for about 40 years, he still retains his enchanting Italian accent that draws you in as he welcomes you to the restaurant and guides you to your table, or as he recommends dishes and describes the daily specials. It's this kind of homely charm that has attracted a very loyal crowd. Not many restaurants can boast regulars who have returned on a weekly basis for over nine years.

The home-like style is also evident in the décor. The restaurant is located in a shophouse, and the owner is careful to redecorate every year, citing that a change keeps the place fresh. This keeps guests from

THIS PAGE (FROM TOP): The restaurant offers diners a chance to savour a taste of Italy; the ground floor can seat up to 60 people at once.

OPPOSITE (FROM TOP): Each dish is not only painstakingly prepared, it is also carefully laid out and garnished before being presented to the diner; the interior is decorated with vibrant colours that contribute to the warm atmosphere.

becoming bored, and yet does not diminish the restaurant's cosiness. Along with the shophouse setting and the traditional Italian cuisine, the annual revamp of its interior makes Pasta Brava an extremely attractive dining option. This is enhanced by the eclectic selection of vivid paintings and antique furnishings that are scattered all over.

But the most important element here, as it is in any other dining establishment, is the food. Pasta Brava specialises in authentic, deeply traditional Italian food made the way it has always been done at home in Italy. It's the kind of delicious comfort food that keeps diners coming back when the chichi and trendy just won't cut it.

What you will find on the menu is a rich selection of authentic dishes, with a freshness you can rely on, safe in the knowledge that all the pasta is made in the kitchen. For starters, try the *calamari* or the *antipasto della casa*, which consists of a selection of grilled vegetables. Moving on to the pasta course, perhaps the most famous is the spaghetti *pescatore al nero di seppia*, spaghetti cooked with seafood and squid ink. This dish may look messy but should be tried at least once. You may even find yourself hooked! Hidden in the dark ink is a generous helping of scallop, shrimp and crayfish, and the taste is just salty enough to bring to mind the ocean. Most accept the unsightly black teeth, as the dish is simply too delicious to forgo, but if you're worried about your white shirt, use one of the bibs.

Other pasta specialities here include the *manicotti ripieni di zucca* (pumpkin ravioli) and *stracci ai gamberi e capesante* (seafood pasta with saffron cream sauce). For the main course, the *filetto di manzo al vino rosso and cioccolato* (steak with red wine-and-chocolate sauce) is a somewhat unusual combination that really works. Of course, it is imperative that you leave room for dessert. The amaretto *panna cotta* has many adoring fans, and the *tiramisu* is a perennial favourite.

The restaurant is split into two floors; upstairs is a room for 50 people and a private bar, a perfect option for celebrations and parties. Pasta Brava is also great for a quiet dinner, a weekend lunch or an intimate dinner for two. In short, everyone needs a Pasta Brava in their life; it's just like coming home.

seats
110

food
classic Italian

drink
Italian wine

features
top floor converts into function room with private bar

nearby
Chinatown • Tanjong Pagar MRT station

contact
11 Craig Road, Tanjong Pagar, Singapore 089671 • telephone: +65.6227 7550 • facsimile: +65.6734 4119 • email: info@pastabrava.com.sg • website: www.pastabrava.com.sg

senso ristorante + bar

THIS PAGE: Stylish contemporary décor sets the stage for fine cuisine from the kitchen of the restaurant's talented chef.

OPPOSITE (FROM LEFT): The courtyard is ideal for intimate gatherings of friends who wish to savour dinner and a glass of wine; apart from the delectable tiramisu, an array of other sugary confections are also served here, including slices of mouthwatering lemon tart.

Senso Ristorante & Bar is an eight-year old establishment in Club Street which provides world-class Italian dining.

Its Executive Chef is a native of Italy whose cooking experience and extensive knowledge comes from kitchens all over Europe. Working in collaboration with him is the General Manager, who chooses the best wine to complement the fine cuisine.

One of the many innovative dishes the restaurant offers is pan-fried cod fillet served with boiled rosemary potatoes in aged balsamico and extra virgin olive oil sauce. Dessert aficionados must try the *tiramisu*, based on the chef's own family recipe. Set menus are available for groups of 12 or more. These menus are updated regularly: the set lunch menu is changed on a weekly basis while the set dinner menu is revised every month—all the more reason to make frequent visits so as to ensure you don't miss a thing.

Inside, there is a beautiful private room that accommodates up to 25 guests at once—very popular for intimate events such as wedding receptions and business meetings. Before or after their meals, diners can enjoy a signature grappa at the luminous bar, or lounge in the sleek leather sofas near it.

It has possibly the largest selection of Super Tuscan wines in Singapore...

seats
restaurant: 120 • courtyard: 40 • bar: 40 •
combined standing room for 400

food
contemporary Italian

drink
extensive wine list • bar

features
private room • courtyard

nearby
Chinatown • Tanjong Pagar • Ann Siang Hill •
Central Business District

contact
21 Club Street, Singapore 069410 •
telephone: +65.6224 3534 •
facsimile: +65.6224 5508 •
email: senso@singnet.com.sg •
website: www.senso.sg

There are over 250 wines stored in Senso Ristorante & Bar's walk-in temperature-controlled cellar. It has possibly the largest selection of Super Tuscan wines in Singapore, including Tignanello, Solaia, Ornellaia and Sassicaia. The extensive wine list consists of both old and new world labels, vintages from Gaja and Antinori, and perhaps the oldest Barolo in Southeast Asia—the 1924 Barolo Borgogno Reserved.

Outside is a patio with a reproduction of a Michelangelo sculpture. Laid-back yet elegant, this space has been carefully designed to resemble a Tuscan courtyard.

Ever since its grand opening in 2000, Senso Ristorante & Bar has earned several awards and much recognition for its cuisine, restaurant design and exemplary service from the World Gourmet Summit, *Wine & Dine Magazine*, *Singapore Tatler*, *Wine & Dine Guide* and *The Wine Review*. It has also been named the 'top-rated Italian restaurant in Singapore' in *Asia Tatler*'s Regional Best Restaurants Guide.

The word 'senso', which is Italian for 'senses', embodies *la dolce vita*—the excellent company of friends is meant to be cherished in the same way that good food and wine are meant to be consumed: at an unhurried pace.

Reservations are encouraged at Senso Ristorante & Bar, which is open for lunch and dinner on weekdays, for dinner on Saturdays, and for brunch on Sundays. Some guests may also be pleased to discover that the restaurant has a sister outlet in Geneva.

aroundtheisland

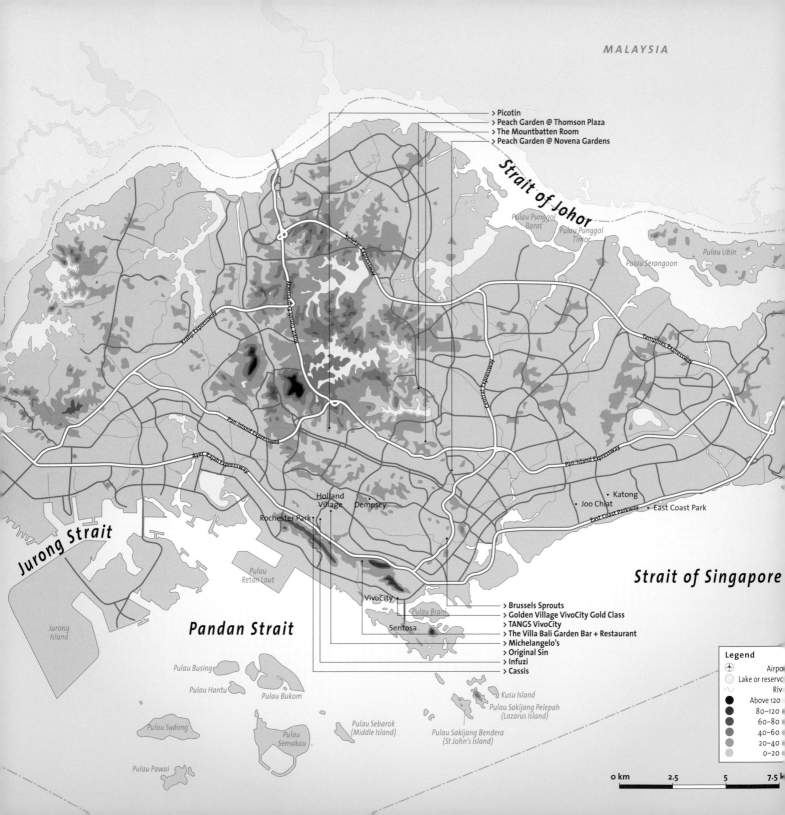

MALAYSIA

Strait of Johor

Strait of Singapore

Jurong Strait

Pandan Strait

> Picotin
> Peach Garden @ Thomson Plaza
> The Mountbatten Room
> Peach Garden @ Novena Gardens

Pulau Punggol Barat
Pulau Punggol Timor
Pulau Serangoon
Pulau Ubin

Seletar Expressway
Central Expressway
Tampines Expressway
Kranji Expressway
Pan-Island Expressway
Ayer Rajah Expressway
East Coast Parkway

Katong
Joo Chiat
East Coast Park

Holland Village
Dempsey
Rochester Park

VivoCity
Pulau Brani
Sentosa

> Brussels Sprouts
> Golden Village VivoCity Gold Class
> TANGS VivoCity
> The Villa Bali Garden Bar + Restaurant
> Michelangelo's
> Original Sin
> Infuzi
> Cassis

Jurong Island

Pulau Retan Laut

Pulau Busing
Pulau Hantu
Pulau Bukom
Pulau Sudong
Pulau Semakau
Pulau Pawai

Pulau Sebarok (Middle Island)

Kusu Island
Pulau Sakijang Pelepah (Lazarus Island)
Pulau Sakijang Bendera (St John's Island)

Legend

⊕ Airpo[rt]
◯ Lake or reservo[ir]
〜 Riv[er]
● Above 120
● 80–120
● 60–80
● 40–60
● 20–40
● 0–20

o km   2.5   5   7.5 k[m]

around the island

Singapore's cosmopolitan city centre and the ethnic areas of Chinatown, Arab Street and Little India routinely attract the most number of visitors. However, they are just part of the many delights that the island has to offer. The irresistible blend of ethnic flavours and the sophistication of an international city means that there's plenty to do and see outside the limits of the city centre.

Given Singapore's compact size and extremely well-planned infrastructure, most destinations are about a 15-minute drive away. This ensures that the most interesting places are never too far away. Go on and wander around the island, and you will find pockets of culture and entertainment, exquisite clothes and antiques, and of course, some of the best culinary offerings in Singapore.

katong + joo chiat

One of the most charming neighbourhoods in the country, Katong is a heritage area that holds a special place in the hearts of many Singaporeans. In the early 19th century, Katong and neighbouring Joo Chiat were largely coconut plantations dotted with humble village homes. In the 1920s and 1930s, many communities moved eastward, away from the city centre, and settled in these areas, transforming them into residential neighbourhoods.

The prominence of Straits Chinese, or Peranakans, and Eurasians among those who moved to these areas lent Katong and Joo Chiat a special charm, still seen in shophouses that line the streets. You can taste the distinct flavour of Peranakan cuisine and see the remaining craftsmen who, true to their traditional art, still make bead slippers and ornate *kebaya* blouses by hand.

dempsey + rochester + tanglin village

Urban development in Singapore has always focused on infusing modern elements into older areas rather than building new neighbourhoods. The result is the creation of delightful clusters like Tanglin Village and Dempsey Hill, as well as the transformation of lesser-known places such as Wessex Estate and Rochester Park, into choice destinations for shopping and dining.

Dempsey Hill was once known for the British army barracks that lined the area. Today, the area sports a stretch of antique shops, fashion houses and galleries, as well as a good collection of restaurants and bars. Rochester Park too had a link with the British army; its prominent black-and-white bungalows were designated as homes for British army officers. Today, these same bungalows house some of the best dining establishments on the island. Dempsey Hill and Rochester Park bring together nostalgic, old-world charm with lush greenery—the perfect setting for the many shops and restaurants in the area.

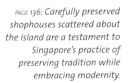

PAGE 136: Carefully preserved shophouses scattered about the island are a testament to Singapore's practice of preserving tradition while embracing modernity.

THIS PAGE: A fierce stone lion stands guard outside a Peranakan-style shophouse in Joo Chiat. Such statues are believed to guard the home or building against evil spirits.

THIS PAGE (FROM TOP): *An example of the award-winning Italian cuisine at Michelangelo's; the contemporary interior of Capella Singapore, a luxury hotel coming up at Sentosa.*

OPPOSITE: *The beaches on Sentosa draw many visitors with the promise of pristine white sands and clear waters.*

holland village

Even before Tanglin Village, Dempsey Hill or Rochester Park became prominent, Holland Village was already known as the premier entertainment and dining alternative to downtown Singapore. Catering to a large number of expatriates who chose to settle in the vicinity, Holland Village became a self-contained enclave of shopping and dining options. Holland Village's best feature is its alfresco sidewalk cafés, interspersed between trendy restaurants and bars.

sentosa

Sentosa, located south of Singapore, was once used by the British as a military and naval base. The island has since been converted into a mini-getaway. Some of the attractions range from historic tours at Fort Siloso with its 17th-century cannons, to Underwater World Singapore with over 250 species of fish, and the Sentosa 4D Magix theatre with special 'live' effects. The island's greenery makes it a natural spot for fine golf courses, including the Sentosa Golf Club, which is regarded as one of the top five golf facilities in Asia. Sentosa is also popular among sun-worshippers—with a choice of three white-sanded beaches, and some of the best bars dotting their landscape, there is no dearth of choice.

Several new hotels and resorts are expected in the near future—a notable one being Capella Singapore. Designed by Pritzker Prize Laureate Lord Norman Foster, the hotel is centred around two restored colonial buildings called the Tanah Merah. Built in the 1880s by the British military, the Tanah Merah served as entertainment centres. Housed in these historic buildings, Capella Singapore will offer both modern luxury and old-world charm.

others

Next to Harbourfront, the entry point to Sentosa, stands VivoCity, Singapore's largest mall to date. VivoCity offers luxury shopping and dining options, a rooftop park, an amphitheatre and cinemas. It even houses artworks by six internationally renowned artists.

a different side of singapore

Traipse about the old shophouses of Katong and Joo Chiat, explore the entertainment enclaves in Dempsey Hill and Holland Village, or stroll along the beaches at Sentosa—there are a variety of experiences waiting to entrance you and reveal different facets of this compact island-state.

...a variety of experiences waiting to entrance you...

restaurants + bars + cafés

katong + joo chiat

Katong, Joo Chiat and the nearby area of Geylang have earned the loyalty of food aficionados for a good reason—the best in Nyonya dumplings and durian puffs are to be found here.

In addition, coffeeshops such as the **Chin Mee Chin Confectionary** (204 East Coast Road), saturated with old-world charm, are landmark institutions in this culturally rich neighbourhood.

When in Katong, a bowl of *laksa*—a noodle dish bathed in a thick and spicy coconut gravy—is a must-try. The long-running Katong 'laksa' wars' see many stalls claiming to have the original and the best recipe. Given the rich complexity of coconut milk and a blend of spices used to make the gravy—the star attraction—the fuss is understandable. Most *laksa* connoisseurs agree that the versions at **328 Katong Laksa** (216 East Coast Road) and **Famous 49 Katong Laksa** (49 East Coast Road) are the best. Another noodle dish, *wanton mee*, also has a cult following. **Fei Fei Wanton Mee** (64 Joo Chiat Place) and **Eng's Char Siew Wan Ton Mee** (271 Onan Road) offer springy noodles with a generous serving of chilli sauce and dumplings.

Peranakan-style glutinous rice dumplings have been perfected by the family that runs **Kim Choo Kueh Chang** (60 Joo Chiat Place), an establishment that has been around for over 50 years. Hearty Peranakan cuisine is also served at **Guan Hoe Soon Restaurant** (214 Joo Chiat Road) and **Glory Catering** (139 East Coast Road). For other classics, **Joo Heng Restaurant** (360 Joo Chiat Road) serves up commendable Chinese stirfry dishes, while **Eng Seng Restaurant** (247/249 Joo Chiat Place) is the black pepper crab favourite.

For those with a sweet tooth, durian puffs and cakes from **Puteri Mas** (475 Joo Chiat Road) are the best introduction to the famous local fruit.

rochester park + wessex estate + others

Rochester Park is well known for its select dining options, many of which are housed in colonial bungalows. Balancing style with substance, they have set the bar high for entertainment and dining.

Leading the way are **Da Paolo Bistro Bar** (3 Rochester Park), **Cassis** (7 Rochester Park) and **Min Jiang @ One-North** (5 Rochester Park)— among the best-known names for Italian, French and Chinese cuisines.

Another well-known name, **The Villa Bali Garden Bar & Restaurant** (9 Lock Road, Gillman Village) offers Balinese fare in an authentic setting.

Choices like **Cicada** (7 Portsdown Road), **Laurent's Café and Chocolate Bar** (5B Portsdown Road), and **Pietrasanta** (5B Portsdown Road) ensure that cocktail fans have no lack of choice. often named as one of Singapore's most popular bars, **Klee** (5B Portsdown Road) has perfected the art of bespoke luxury cocktails, with fresh ingredients and innovative mixologists.

THIS PAGE (ANTICLOCKWISE FROM TOP): Lounge in a pavilion at Villa Bali, a Balinese-themed outdoor bar; the breeze offers some relief from the heat at The Verandah café; seafood is often added to laksa to give it more flavour.

OPPOSITE: Cassis serves up fine French cuisine, which probably tastes best when savoured with friends.

restaurants + bars + cafés

dempsey + tanglin village

Jones the Grocer (9 Dempsey Road) and **Culina** (617 Bukit Timah Road) both have bistros within the premises featuring a selection of gourmet cheese, wine, ham and desserts for hearty brunches and dinners.

The **Karma Kettle Café & Wine Bistro** (501 Bukit Timah Road) brings old-school charm back to life. A retro-colonial restaurant and wine bistro, it serves traditional European recipes in a rustic yet cosy setting.

Housed in a bungalow brimming with nostalgic charm, **Au Petit Salut** (40C Harding Road) has won many accolades for its French cuisine.

The **PS Café**'s (28B Harding Road) famous Sunday brunch has made it one of the most popular restaurants in the area. Alternatively, plan your Sunday brunch around perfect pancakes and eggs benedict at the open-air **Riders' Café** (Bukit Timah Saddle Club), or watch a polo game in comfort while you breakfast on local and Western delights at **The Verandah** (Singapore Polo Club).

Some of the best bars are found in the leafy hills around Dempsey Road. Be it **Hacienda**'s (13A Dempsey Road) intimate outdoor bar, the stunning sophistication of **Oosh** (22 Dempsey Road) or the laid-back vibes of the **Wine Network** (Block 13 Dempsey Road), there are choices aplenty for the discerning.

holland village

Holland Village's finest restaurants are Italian joints **Michelangelo's**, (Block 44 Jalan Merah Saga), **Sistina Ristorante** (Block 44 Jalan Merah Saga) and **Original Sin** (Block 43 Jalan

THIS PAGE (FROM TOP): The Japanese chefs at Nogawa work hard to whip up culinary delights for diners; the intimate interiors of Infuzi make it a great place for a date.
OPPOSITE (FROM LEFT): At Golden Village VivoCity Gold Class, fare such as this enticing Gold Class Burger is just a push of a button away, even while the movie is screening; watch the sunset from the comfort of a daybed at Cafe del Mar.

Merah Saga). Original Sin stands out as the best—and only—upscale, fully vegetarian restaurant in the country.

Enjoy sidewalk dining at Holland Village with authentic Lebanese at **Al Hamra Lebanese & Middle Eastern Cuisine** (23 Lorong Mambong) and hearty Italian at **La Nonna** (26/26B Lorong Mambong). Or pick up freshly baked breads and light pastries from the Japanese-French **Provence Bakery** (17A Lorong Liput). Dessert-lovers will surely appreciate the spread at **2am: Dessert Bar** (21A Lorong Liput).

The **Wala Wala Café and Bar** (31 Lorong Mambong) has a strong following among live-music lovers. House regulars Shirlyn & The UnXpected typically play a mix of rock covers and original scores. **Baden Baden Restaurant & Pub**'s (42 Lorong Mambong) main draw is Bavarian beer, while **Turn:Styles** (17C Lorong Liput) is the best place for a night of football-watching or a game of pool.

A neighbourhood bistro, **Sweet Salty Spicy** (392 Upper Bukit Timah Road) serves up modern Thai with a touch of Australian. For Italian and French fare, **Ristorante Da Valentino** (11 Jalan Bingka) and **Picotin** (100 Turf Club Road), respectively are among the best choices.

Island Creamery (10 Jalan Serene) offers homemade ice cream with local flavours—a choice worth mentioning is the Tiger Beer sorbet, best enjoyed after a gourmet burger at **Relish** (501 Bukit Timah Road).

sentosa

Sentosa is home to some of the best dining options, led by top restaurants **The Cliff** (Sentosa Resort & Spa) and

Nogawa Restaurant (Sentosa Golf Club), which specialise in French and Japanese cuisines respectively.

Several restaurants at Sentosa offer a classic combination—gourmet cuisine with a view. Enjoy the view of the Straits of Singapore as you tuck in to perfectly executed Italian classics at **il Lido**. The cold seafood platter at the beach-side **Barnacles** (Rasa Sentosa Resort) has won several accolades. In addition, the panoramic view of the South China Sea adds to the overall dining experience. With the picturesque sunset by the beach, and a choice of well-prepared cocktails, an evening at **Café Del Mar** (Siloso Beach) is not to be missed.

The **Suburbia** (30 Allanbrooke Road) offers quality wines in a classy setting, while the waterfront **Privé** (2 Keppel Bay Vista) has a café, restaurant and bar, with views of the yachts at the Keppel Bay Marina.

others

Movie-buffs will love the **Golden Village Gold Class** (VivoCity), where reclining seats and personalised service have brought new levels of luxury to the experience of watching a movie.

shopping

katong + joo chiat

Katong Antique House (208 East Coast Road) provides glimpses into the past through costumes, furniture and crockery that were once part of a traditional Peranakan household. Not far away, **Rumah Bebe** (113 East Coast Road) continues the tradition of handmade beaded slippers and embroidered bags. Here you have the rare option of having a Peranakan artisan custom make an item for you.

One of the many boutiques tucked away among the houses is **The Lawn** (38 Ean Kiam Place), which carries clothes and accessories for men and women. Shop at **EggThree** (260 Joo Chiat Road) for fashionable jewellery or home accessories, and take home a couple of pieces as gifts.

dempsey road

Dempsey Road is an idyllic enclave of lifestyle and art. Art galleries and antique shops are aplenty, alongside gourmet grocery stores.

For connoisseurs of cheese, **Jones the Grocer** (Block 9, Dempsey Road) offers a hundred artisanal farmhouse cheeses from France, Wales and Australia in its famed cheese room.

Art-lovers must make it a point to explore **Linda Gallery** (Block 15, Dempsey Road), reputed for its collection of Chinese contemporary art. Here, you are sure to find a worthy piece to grace your home.

holland village

If you are a food enthusiast, Holland Village is a good place for you. Pick up exquisite kitchenware and cookbooks at **Pantry Magic** (43 Jalan Merah Saga), and shop for organic food products at **Bunalun** (43 Jalan Merah Saga). Drop by **Shermay's Cooking School** (43 Jalan Merah Saga) for baking accessories and cookbooks, and even sign up for their cooking classes.

If you are looking to spruce up your home's décor, pick up accessories at **Lim's Arts and Crafts** (211 Holland Avenue). For a pick of colourful home furnishings, or intricately carved silverware and jewellery, head to **Este'h Studio** (211 Holland Avenue).

others

For fashionable clothes and accessories or home décor items, head to **TANGS VivoCity**.

If you are closer to the city centre, head to Robertson Walk, and look for **Bodhi Art Gallery** (11 Unity Street) Featuring artworks and sculptures by Indian artists, this a good place to invest in art.

THIS PAGE (CLOCKWISE FROM TOP): Carved silver boxes from Este'h Studio; purchase a pair of classy shoes or a handbag from TANGS VivoCity; choose from an array of cheeses and wines from gourmet stores.

OPPOSITE (CLOCKWISE FROM TOP): Rumah Bebe showcases the Peranakan arts; EggThree's home accessories will add a touch of class to your abode; Bodhi Art Gallery is the place to go to view art by Indian artists.

PAGE 148: Chinese Garden's carefully sculpted greenery and vintage architectural style are a must-see.

golden village vivocity gold class

THIS PAGE: Five-star cuisine, dedicated service and the most comfortable seating available in local cinemas—what more do you need for the ultimate luxury movie experience?

OPPOSITE (FROM TOP): The Gold Class lounge is decked out in shades of red, grey, cream and brown; dine in comfort while watching the latest movie in the Gold Class cinemas.

Going to the cinema in Singapore stepped up a notch or three with the introduction of Gold Class at the Golden Village Cineplex. Here, cinema-goers can relax in ultimate luxury while taking in the latest blockbuster.

Each viewing hall houses electronically controlled recliner seats that have in-built call buttons; the spacious and plush chairs are made even cosier with a blanket that blocks out chilly air-conditioning. Fast and discreet attention is assured with a butler service, so you get the food and drink you want without missing any part of the film. Think first-class travel on the best airline and you're on the right track, only this is no tiny screen you're looking at—the wide screens stretch from wall to wall, and are accompanied by Dolby Digital surround sound.

The Gold Class experience can be found at Golden Village Grand at Great World City and at Golden Village VivoCity, but the latter has taken it two notches higher with its five-star fine-dining menu and formidable wine list. Two experienced chefs, Executive Chef Chris Foo and Chef de Cuisine Ronnie Ng, work together to create a menu that serves to enhance the luxe atmosphere.

Dishes on the menu include the crispy duck leg confit, which comes in an orange reduction alongside seasonal vegetables and potatoes. The chicken *shashlik* skewers are flavoured with a fragrant lavender emulsion, and accompanied by a mesclun mix and potato wedges. Other popular dishes include the Gold Class Burger—170 g (6 oz) of prime beef with delicious relish—and Golden Wings. The set lunch and dinner consist of an appetiser, main course and dessert, and will see you right through the movie.

If you prefer, you can dine in the lounge before or after the film is screened. This luxurious, spacious area can easily host over a hundred people at once. Thirsty? You can order a little something to go with your meal from the Gold Class bar, which has an impressive beverage list that includes award-winning fine wine. Yabby Lake Australian wine and Valt Scottish malt whiskey are popular favourites amongst patrons.

...relax in ultimate luxury while taking in the latest blockbuster.

seats
VivoCity Gold Class: 24-seat theatre,
38-seat theatre, 48-seat theatre ·
Grand Gold Class: 30-seat theatre

food
international · themed menus

drink
extensive wine list · cocktails

features
themed evenings · fully reclining seats ·
call buttons on seats · private parties ·
corporate functions · personal butler service

nearby
Harbourfront Centre · St James Power Station ·
Singapore Cruise Centre · shops

contact
GV VivoCity: No 1 Harbourfront Walk,
#02-30 VivoCity, Singapore 098585 ·
GV Grand: 1 Kim Seng Promenade,
#03-39/40 Great World City, Singapore 237994 ·
telephone: +65.6311 9162 ·
facsimile: +65.6334 8397 ·
email: customersvc@goldenvillage.com.sg ·
website: www.gv.com.sg

The menu changes regularly and the chefs mark occasions with special themes. For example, Valentine's Day is celebrated with a bottle of champagne. Certain menus are inspired by films—Mamma Mia! for example had its own Greek-style menu. Past events, such as the Singapore Food Festival, had local specialities such as chilli crab and *chendol* making a special appearance on the menu.

It's a wonder that there are not more of these little (or not-so-little) movie hideouts around. However, it's this sense of exclusivity that keeps it special. For those who love experiencing movies in the cinema, the Gold Class will change your thinking forever. Somehow, the chime of glasses and the clinking of cutlery on china is much easier to take than the constant rustling of sweet papers and interminable munching of popcorn, especially with the added bonus of a huge amount of space to yourself. And, as with the best in anything, once you have tried it, it's impossible to settle for anything less. Bravo Golden Village.

brussels sprouts

One would imagine that after working so long and hard over his other restaurants, Chef Emmanuel Stroobant wanted a place where he could kick back and have some fun. And in that, Brussels Sprouts does not disappoint.

This cosy little restaurant is located right at the heart of the trendy Robertson Quay area. Facing the Singapore River and just a short stroll away from several pubs and a number of other establishments meant for fun and relaxation, this mussels joint is a break from the norm.

Most of the seating is alfresco with high benches and bar stools giving the place an edgy feel. However, guests who prefer air-conditioning can sit inside, where lower dining tables are available. The walls are painted a cheerful yellow and the Tintin mural completes the look. Lighting the inside are several unusual Perspex two-dimensional bulbs that seem to hang in the air without support. As a whole, this restaurant and bar is an über-chic affair. On the fun side of rowdy, it is a great place to go with mates, especially on weekends.

THIS PAGE: Guests can choose to sit inside, surrounded by cheerful yellow walls and bright lights, or outside, on tall bar stools and high benches.

OPPOSITE: Mussels are invariably presented with Belgian fries.

...the menu speaks for itself.

The menu is divided into Small Eats, Garden Eats and Platters, Mussels, Big Eats, Side Eats and Sweet Eats. Belgian specialities are evident throughout but visitors may want to pay extra attention to the Small Eats, featuring delicious grey shrimp croquettes, rollmops (pickled herring) on toast and ham, caper and gherkin salad.

The star of the show has to be the mussels. Taking up a whole page of the three-page menu, there are no less than 24 different ways to serve a pot of fresh mussels. The sauce can be clear, creamy, local or gratinated. Some examples of traditional flavours are *moules marinières* and *moules Provençales*; or perhaps guests would like to try the Belgian special, *moules à la Leffe Blonde*. Local-style preparations on the menu include Chinese, which consists of ginger, sesame oil and *shao hsing* wine; Imperial, where the sauce is a double-boiled chicken stock with ginseng, red dates and wolfberries; and Devilled, a hot and spicy sauce made with chilli padi, coriander, curry, lime and tomato. Mussels are served with Belgian fries as a matter of course, which come in brightly coloured plastic 'buckets' that are refilled by the watchful staff. Dip them in the homemade mayonnaise and try not to get lost in food-heaven.

It is impossible to forget the Sweet Eats. Classic vanilla-flavoured *crème brulée*, banana *crêpe* with a butterscotch sauce, Belgian chocolate mousse, Belgian chocolate cake, Belgian waffles—the menu speaks for itself.

The bar has a whopping 120 different Belgian beers on its list—Brussels Sprouts's *pièce de résistance*. Some of these beers are extremely difficult to find, in Singapore or anywhere outside of Belgium. The list includes light and fruity as well as malty full-bodied varieties; there is even a cherry champagne-flavoured beer. Be careful though, some are very strong—the most 'lethal' at Brussels Sprouts is Bush Amber. At 12 per cent, it is the strongest Belgian beer on the market.

So, for a casual evening, Brussels Sprouts is a winner. It's a hip and well-thought out establishment in terms of look, feel, service and food, and clearly a stayer on Singapore's otherwise fickle restaurant scene.

seats
250

food
Belgian · mussels

drink
Belgian beer

features
children eat for free · magic shows Saturday night and Sunday at lunch · alfresco dining

nearby
Robertson Quay · Boat Quay · Central · Clarke Quay

contact
80 Mohammed Sultan Road, #01-12 The Pier@Robertson, Singapore 239013 · telephone: +65.6887 4344 · facsimile: +65.6887 4144 · email: info@brusselssprouts.com.sg · website: www.brusselssprouts.com.sg

cassis

THIS PAGE: Step through the inviting entrance encircled by palm fronds and take a moment to drink in the stunning sight of Cassis' exterior and kitchen before allowing the smartly dressed staff to show you to a table.

OPPOSITE: On a cool evening, guests may wish to enjoy a romantic dinner seated outdoors, in the midst of glowing arches and the sweet fragrance of flowers.

In 2006, an enclave of colonial bungalows dating back to the 1940s—affectionately known among locals as the 'Black and Whites' for their uniform façades of white walls with black supports—were transformed into Rochester Park, an elegant lifestyle development shrouded in luxuriant vegetation. Just minutes away from Holland Village, the secluded estate paints a quiet picture of Singapore that many visitors dream of, but few find among the glimmering avenues of modernity that have emerged everywhere else across the island.

The establishments occupying Rochester Park's limited number of addresses represent the *crème de la crème* of retail and dining. Each builds upon the old-world backdrop with richly realised European décor schemes, drawing admirers and cool-hunters from around the globe.

This atmosphere has proven to be a perfect setting for Cassis, a superlative French restaurant in an increasingly affluent society distinguished by some of the highest achievements in modern gastronomy. Amidst

the rambling gardens and verdant foliage thick with the sounds of a tropical rainforest—an unusual setting for this type of restaurant—its fine dining approach is far from where most diners' expectations may lie. However, as the authentic flavours reveal themselves, diners will find the enchanting location perfectly copacetic.

For those wishing to host a dinner event, the 279-sq m (3,000-sq ft) bungalow and the landscaped estate can be converted into a function venue that easily accommodates up to 200. The grounds measure more than 1,951 sq m (21,000 sq ft) and serve as the alfresco dining area. There is also a separate bar area where guests can indulge in pre- and post-dinner drinks from sunset to midnight. All through the property, smart design cues tie the stylish interiors and spacious dining hall to the building's historical roots, while well-considered outdoor lighting imbues the entire space with an air of romance and intimacy.

Three discrete environments constitute the outdoor seating options. The first is a sunken pavilion with two long rows of plush seating separated by a formidable table, under a majestic patterned tent that seems to be have been borne out of a meeting between French and Arab artists. The second is a tiered patio beneath a series of lit arches adorned with frangipani, with a shimmering glass ceiling above it all. Lastly, those desiring a clearer view of the night sky may prefer a seat out on the open terrace, where nature

can be clearly seen, heard and felt. These spaces are ideal for both small and large groups, but parties may opt for one of two private dining rooms on the second floor that seat 10 and 12 respectively.

Patrons come to Cassis to experience an interpretation of traditional French recipes and cooking methods filtered through the lens of contemporary demands and first-rate ingredients. Behind all this is a chef as renowned for his perfectionism as he is for his self-taught rise through the ranks of the Michelin list. The results of his culinary genius are available six days a week.

THIS PAGE: *The sleek interiors are decorated in a bold black-and-white scheme, with touches of crimson adding spice to the overall visual effect.*

OPPOSITE: *With the help of his capable team, Chef Guilbert produces creations that stimulate all of one's senses.*

Eric Guilbert heads the Food & Beverage division of Cassis's parent company, and also plays the part of Executive Chef in its dynamic open kitchen. He began his career 19 years ago at the age of 15, spending several years in some of the best restaurants in Paris, including Drouant and Tour d'Argent. On a red letter day in 2000, the noted critic Fay Maschler dined at London's Admiralty restaurant, where Chef Guilbert was serving as head chef, and proclaimed it—and its talented leader—one of the most gratifying discoveries of the decade. A tour of Asia followed soon after, with appointments at the Park Lane Hotel in Jakarta, Sookmyung Academy's Le Cordon Bleu in Seoul and the Oberoi Hotel in Lombok. In between those dates came a Michelin star in Spain for his tenure as the Executive Chef of the Lido, at the Las Dunas Beach Hotel & Spa.

The level of innovation and craft that Chef Guilbert brings to Cassis is apparent when one peruses the modest but varied menu. That sense rises sharply as the delicately plated meals approach the table. In signature creations such as the red mullet fillet served with potato gnocchi and asparagus spears, the chef reveals a confident touch tempered by years of thinking on his feet. The fish is exquisitely prepared and comes with an accompaniment of lemongrass and a white wine sauce with shallots that reveal further depth and character in the flavour of the dish.

Another favourite is the duck liver terrine with a sweet fig marmalade, port jelly and almond brioche. If guests are in the mood for some meat, there is the leg of lamb, which is slow-cooked for seven hours before being served alongside a truffle-infused potato purée and freshly made butter. Alternatively, a lamb shoulder pan-seared with pancetta, flageolet beans, vegetables and rosemary sauce offers a more piquant take on the meat. Other must-try dishes include the roasted pigeon with soya and Xeres vinegar, and of course, the signature *foie gras* set off against a refreshingly tart raspberry sauce.

If Eric Guilbert and his modern cuisine are the stars of Cassis, then the auteur behind the scenes is most certainly Mahesh Ramnani, its CEO and co-founder. Raised and educated in many different countries before emerging as a luminary of the Baltic states, the nonconformist entrepreneur owns, among other things, an international Cuban cigar distribution business built upon his love of smoking. In the case of Cassis, he was driven by his passion for fine food. The impresario has imbued the eatery with a dash of the same *je ne sais quoi* that surrounds him. From the moment one arrives, to the warm parting words offered by the staff as one leaves, there's a completeness to every visit that can only come from the guidance of accomplished management.

By virtue of its exclusive location alone, Cassis is a place where connoisseurs of French cuisine can combine their love for fine dining with an appreciation for historic architecture and the great outdoors. What everyone eventually takes away is a private memory of an unforgettable dining experience.

seats
dinner events: 200 • cocktail events: 500

food
classic French prepared using modern techniques

drink
bar • wine list

features
outdoor dining amidst gardens • private dining rooms • valet parking • private or corporate events

nearby
Rochester Park • Holland Village • Buona Vista MRT Station

contact
7 Rochester Park, Singapore 139217 • telephone: +65.6872 9366 • facsimile: +65.6872 6071 • email: info@capriceholdings.net • website: www.cassis.com.sg

infuzi

THIS PAGE: *White dominates the interior, giving the restaurant an airy and spacious feel.*

OPPOSITE: *Every dish produced in the kitchens, from the smallest starter to the daintiest dessert, is a product of Chef Lee's years of experience and his own creative flair with ingredients.*

Singaporeans are said to enjoy searching for good food almost as much as eating it. Of course, in a country like Singapore—densely populated and completely urbanised, with no shortage of tiny hidden eateries and a robust restaurant industry that sees the opening of new establishments as quickly as trends arrive—there's no doubt that hunting builds up quite the appetite. Even when armed with the advice of local experts and the habit of interviewing strangers on the street, there are some names that one might never hear; too unique or special to be freely mentioned, they remain well-guarded secrets to reward truly inquisitive and dedicated gourmands.

Infuzi is one such treasure, situated at so unlikely an address that accidental discoveries are almost inconceivable. Whether its owners intended to cultivate secrecy or simply fell in love with the bright, glass-walled space that offers views of lush greenery is up for debate. However, the fact remains that operating out of a unit in the Biopolis—a cluster of buildings housing biotechnology and medical science companies—has granted Infuzi something of an outsider status among the island's fine-dining establishments. Despite being hard to find, the modern European restaurant is surprisingly easy to get to from the popular Holland Village enclave—a short five-minute drive is all it takes to be transported into a completely different culinary landscape.

Once found, Infuzi is a welcoming affair with both indoor and alfresco seating. The interior combines simple, white low-backed chairs and other minimalist furnishings with some Baroque elements. Some examples of the latter include a huge wall-mounted mirror and curious chandeliers made of empty wine bottles. On the whole, the effect is a tasteful ambience that is both comfortable and unpretentious, much like the food.

...a tasteful ambience that is both comfortable and unpretentious...

seats
indoor: 40 · outdoor: 20

food
modern French with Asian elements

drink
wine list

features
alfresco dining · private events ·
complimentary corkage nights

nearby
Holland Village · Buona Vista MRT station

contact
10 Biopolis Road, #01-01 Chromos Block,
Singapore 138670 ·
telephone: +65.6478 9091 ·
facsimile: +65.6478 9021 ·
email: purdey@infuzi.com.sg ·
website: www.infuzi.com.sg

Chef-owner Freddie Lee's signature dishes are inspired by French cooking and traditional techniques, but incorporate Asian flavours as a subtle twist to each recipe. After spending a decade in the kitchens of the renowned Les Amis—considered home to the country's finest French food—he decided to strike out on his own, and in 2004, Infuzi was born. Chef Lee has taken on the most-loved aspects of his mentor Justin Quek's style and refined it for his new audience, creating another venue that adventurous foodies may wish to seek out.

With perennial favourites such as mud crab cake with black pepper dressing; duck liver accompanied by a port reduction, grapes, mesclun salad and pastry; Maine lobster pasta drizzled with lobster oil and seaweed; and *bouillabaisse* (traditional French seafood stew featuring seasonal fish, prawns, scallops and lobster), Chef Lee has distilled the essence of French and Asian cuisines. Aside from these constants, the menu is changed every three months, offering new combinations of flavours to diners' taste buds.

A three-course set meal is available for lunch. This menu rotates on a weekly basis, so guests can visit regularly without risking boredom. Dinner, on the other hand, is taken care of by a wonderfully balanced six-course tasting menu. It effortlessly covers everything from fresh-caught seasonal seafood to a carefully prepared veal cheek in Madeira sauce—perfect for those who love sampling a variety of foods at one sitting.

Infuzi may prove to be a challenging dining venue to find, but as any Singaporean will tell you, that just makes the meal at the end of the journey even tastier.

michelangelo's

THIS PAGE: *Wall paintings inspired by the restaurant's namesake set the scene for a good meal.*

OPPOSITE: *Vegetarians and diners with special dietary requests need not go hungry—there are alternatives that are as tasty as the rest of the dishes.*

Holland Village has long been a favourite expatriate haunt in Singapore, but its fine restaurants, cafés, delis and boutiques have extended the enclave's appeal to everyone else. The Chip Bee Gardens area is lined with a parade of restaurants and right at the heart of it all is Michelangelo's.

This Italian restaurant first opened its doors in 1995. Chef Angelo Sanelli, the Culinary Director of the group, was quick to embrace the local cuisine and experiment with a blend of Asian tastes and Italian ingredients. These days, he has the assistance of the Executive Chef of Michelangelo's, Chef David Warren, in creating the innovative dishes.

The restaurant has as much seating outside as it does within; the alfresco option makes Michelangelo's the perfect place for intimate dinners or more relaxed occasions. The awning and the warm, mellow light from candles create a romantic air in the evenings, while powerful fans keep diners comfortable in Singapore's perennial heat and humidity. If you are here for lunch and the sun is beating

down too hard, the interior is equally inviting. Draped ceilings hover over Michelangelo-inspired wall paintings, which are a nod to the restaurant's moniker.

On the menu, the chef's specials include, among others, gravadlax of beef as a starter and penne sambuca as a main course. The former is a thick cut carpaccio of beef tenderloin, brushed with a gravadlax-style marinade, accompanied by a confit of lemon and roasted Roma tomatoes, and finished with a white truffle balsamic sauce. The penne sambuca features fresh tiger prawns sautéed with onion, red chilli, semi-dried tomatoes and baby spinach, and then flamed with fine Italian sambuca, before being tossed in a rose sauce with penne pasta.

Other dishes on the menu that draw diners into returning time and again are the eggplant tower, *calamari fritti*, chilli mussels and the popular spaghetti *frutti de mare*, as well as the penne vodka—penne pasta sautéed with onions in clarified butter, flamed with Russian vodka, then drizzled with a rose sauce and topped with fresh parmesan shavings. This, unsurprisingly, is a favourite on the set lunch menu. If you would like something slightly different from how it is presented on the menu, just ask; Chef Sanelli will be happy to make adjustments for you. Diners with special dietary requirements—such as diabetics—also need not worry, as the capable and talented chef is more than able to cook up something special if necessary.

The food is so different here that it's easy to see why Michelangelo's has such a loyal following. But it is not just the food menu, the wine collection is also a huge draw. With over 2,300 labels, the wine menu will satisfy every palate and price range. The wines come from all over the world, including Australia, France, Italy, New Zealand, Spain and the US.

The warm and friendly staff only add to the charm, and have undoubtedly helped the restaurant win many of its local awards and accolades. Some of these include its place as one of the *Wine and Dine Magazine*'s Singapore's Top Restaurants (1997–2007) and the *Wine Spectator*'s Best of Award of Excellence in 2006.

As the flagship of Angelo Sanelli's highly successful Michelangelo's Restaurant group, this gem is a firm favourite for romance. Its alfresco setting and the generally convivial air keep people coming back for more.

seats
indoors: 50 • alfresco: 50

food
Italian

drink
extensive wine list

features
catering services • special events • special menu for diabetics

nearby
Holland Village • Buona Vista MRT station • Queenstown • Holland Road Shopping Centre • Holland V Shopping Mall

contact
Block 44 Jalan Merah Saga, #01-60 Chip Bee Gardens, Singapore 278116 • telephone: +65.6475 9069 • facsimile: +65.6475 4319 • email: reservations@michelangelos.com.sg • website: www.michelangelos.com.sg

original sin

THIS PAGE: *Vibrant colours give the restaurant a cheery air.*

OPPOSITE: *The dishes served here are not only culinary creations that showcase the chef's skill, they are virtually works of art. Be sure to take a moment to appreciate the wonderful presentation before digging in.*

We are all guilty of the original sin, we all give into temptation at one time or another. At this little hideout in the heart of Holland Village, temptation abounds, but only of the non-meat variety. This vegetarian institution is a perennial favourite, and loyal fans keep coming back for more. When it opened its doors to its first guests in 1997, it was Singapore's first vegetarian restaurant and it remains pretty much unchallenged today, barring the occasional Indian restaurant.

Nowhere else in Singapore can you find Mediterranean and Middle Eastern vegetarian cuisine in one restaurant.

Original Sin is a cosy, welcoming place. Its bright sunny entrance, in the daytime, is enhanced by the gigantic mosaic mirror inside. Its open kitchen gives it an even roomier feel and the rustic tiled floors smack of authenticity. Authentic it certainly is. The culinary director—and co-owner—is a Marisa Bertocchi, a vegetarian and an

Australian of Italian descent. She attends to the atmosphere meticulously—she even designed the mosaic piece herself—and ensures that at night the whole place flickers and glitters under candle light.

When it comes to food, Mediterranean fare covers a broad scope. It ranges from Moroccan, Greek and Levantine, to Italian, Spanish and French, allowing for ample inspiration and opportunity for adventurous vegetarian dishes. Emphasis is placed on using only the best and freshest ingredients brought directly from the source.

The specialities at Original Sin include the mezze plate and the *bosco misto*. The former is a quartet of *baba ganoush* (an eggplant dish), *hummus* (mashed and seasoned chickpeas), *tzatziki* (strained yoghurt with cucumber) and the lesser-known *koresh*, a pumpkin and carrot paste infused with caraway and fennel seeds. These much-loved Middle Eastern dips are served with delicious *falafel* patties and warm *pitta* bread. The *bosco misto* is a must-try. The dish comprises patties made of spinach and fetta which are melded with a light tofu. These are then served with sautéed button mushrooms and plum sauce, and topped with fresh asparagus. Perfection!

Another dish that seems to be popular with patrons is the portobello mushroom stuffed with ricotta, spinach, pesto and pine nuts. Once baked it is topped with a tomato-basil sauce and mozzarella cheese—Magic Mushroom is the name of this dish, and it is

certainly appropriate. The *moussaka* (a cooked salad), the vegetarian lasagne and the curries are also highly recommended. With an Italian chef in charge, there are pizzas too but the toppings are less than ordinary with a little Middle Eastern inspiration. Well worth a try.

Located just next door to its brother restaurant, Michelangelo's, wine-lovers can be assured that Original Sin has an excellent wine list, as it shares its collection of wine with its sibling; there are over 2,000 labels from France, Italy, Spain, America, Australia and New Zealand from which to choose.

The restaurant's namesake is the famous Michelangelo painting in the Sistine Chapel, which reflects the artist's passion, creativity and skill. At Original Sin, the cuisine is a reflection of the chef's skill and creativity, and the taste is no less immaculate.

seats
indoor: 40 • outdoor: 40

food
vegetarian Mediterranean

drink
extensive wine list

features
catering services • special events • special menu for vegans and Jain followers

nearby
Holland Village • Buona Vista MRT station • Queenstown • Holland Road Shopping Centre • Holland V Shopping Mall

contact
Block 43 Jalan Merah Saga, #01-62 Chip Bee Gardens, Singapore 278115 • telephone: +65.6475 5605 • facsimile: +65.6475 4416 • email: mgmt@originalsin.com.sg • website: www.originalsin.com.sg

picotin

THIS PAGE: *The warm, mellow lighting highlights the dark glossy wood and pale colours of the restaurant's interior.*

OPPOSITE (FROM TOP): *The covered patio at the back of the restaurant is a good place for those who enjoy some fresh air, natural light and foliage; the fare served here is primarily European but if pasta and breads are not to your taste, there are several other options available.*

Having made his name with the restaurant that is his namesake, Sebastien Reuiller joined forces with Emmanuel Stroobant at the end of 2007. Along with bar manager Jacky Stevens, the talented trio opened a family-oriented establishment that is second to none when it comes to comfort. Based on a clubhouse concept, Picotin is a sanctuary of happy homeliness set in the green expanse of the newly revamped Horse City. Picotin uses much of its natural setting to full advantage—outdoor seating, for instance, allows guests to watch the horses at the nearby riding school while enjoying a meal. Floor-to-ceiling glass windows create a permeability between the green outdoors and the rustic ambience within the restaurant. In addition, the dark wood furniture and classic colour palette evoke a sense of European style.

The managers, Sebastien and Jacky, and their team are always on hand to extend a genuine welcome to guests and usher them to their spot of choice. Friendly service awaits should you wish to have a drink at the bar (to watch a bit of football, or the sport du jour), or enjoy dinner on the covered patio. The kids are not forgotten—young, energetic guests may find that being outside on the grass is their best option, as they can then enjoy a pony ride or have fun in the play area. If a quieter place is preferred, the dining room is also available.

The menu is kept uncomplicated, offering wholesome family fare. Picotin's signature dishes include lobster bisque, duck confit, lamb tagine and, in the dessert menu, all-time favourites such as *crème brulée* and sticky date pudding. Other classics served here are goat's cheese salad, leek-and-parmesan tart and beef stew. The restaurant has its very own wood-fired pizza oven, and the pasta is fresh and homemade. Should guests wish to end their meal with a dessert that is not one of the signature dishes, sweets such as the lemon tart with tamarind and the profiteroles come highly recommended. The children are provided for with the kid's menu, which covers

...a family-oriented establishment that is second to none when it comes to comfort.

seats
bar: 50 · indoor: 40 · outdoor: 120 ·
covered patio: 70

food
classic French, European · pasta · pizza

drink
wine cellar · bar

features
deli · sports on TV · space for functions · bar ·
children's play area · pony rides for children ·
comprehensive children's menu

nearby
riding school · Bukit Timah · Turf City

contact
100 Turf Club Road, Singapore 287992 ·
telephone: +65.6877 1191 ·
facsimile: +65.6877 1141 ·
email: sebastien@picotin.com.sg ·
website: www.picotin.com.sg

breakfast, lunch and dinner. On weekends, diners can even look forward to a barbecue and the proverbial Sunday roast.

The kitchens have flourished under the care of chef Cyrille Springinsfeld, who spent some time in the two Michelin-starred Auberge de la Foret. Chef Springinsfeld is highly skilled in traditional French cooking, and takes pride in every dish under his direction, giving his all to make sure each is perfect.

The wine list will more than suffice to provide an accompaniment to each meal. Sebastien's knowledge of and experience with the subject means that the wine cellar holds a fine selection of old world wine and some new world, mainly from the US and Australia.

Fully intended as a family affair right from the outset, the idea was to bring something of a pastoral feel to Singapore. Surrounded by greenery, with horses grazing nearby, Picotin has become a huge success. In Singapore, where food is such a huge and important part of the local culture, Picotin's offerings woo its customers in just the right way.

For those who prefer to dine at home, Picotin has a new pizza delivery and takeaway service for nearby areas. Beautifully handcrafted meals and accompaniments that add flair to any dinner party can be easily arranged. Just let your fingers do the walking and a sumptuous meal to soothe even the healthiest appetites will soon appear.

the mountbatten room

Spend too long viewing downtown Singapore from the inside of shopping arcades, sleek subway cars and crowded skyscrapers, and you might begin to wonder where everyone goes for a little bit of peace and quiet. Sure, the city's streets may be lined with living colonnades of trees, but the country's other portions of parkland go mostly unnoticed by visitors, save for the Botanic Gardens, perhaps.

Just minutes from the city, the Singapore Polo Club is one such location; it encompasses a little over a hectare (3 acres) of verdant fields off Mount Pleasant Road. Founded in 1886 by Colonial British officers, this private recreation club still retains a nostalgic air that brings to mind a countryside retreat far removed from the typical, hurried pace of life in Singapore.

The club's equestrian and sports facilities are reserved for members. However, the four recently revamped restaurants and bars in the clubhouse are open to the public, and are ideal spots from which to enjoy a cool breeze and the peaceful view over the polo green. With the four establishments now under the direct management of the club (food and beverage operations previously fell to a third

THIS PAGE (FROM TOP): On days when the heat is unbearable, diners may prefer to sit indoors; patrons may wish to watch a game while enjoying a meal or admire the horses as they graze peacefully below.

OPPOSITE (FROM TOP): Order a glass of wine or a refreshing drink to go with the French cuisine; the offerings of Chef Chua's kitchen are not only tasty, they are almost works of art.

party) the Singapore Polo Club is coming into a new phase of its history—that of an eminent dining destination in and of itself.

The jewel of the Polo Club quartet is undoubtedly The Mountbatten Room. The restaurant is named after Lord Louis Mountbatten, under whose auspices the club flourished after World War II. The new interior projects an atmosphere of elegance with crisp white tablecloths and dark earth tones. Bold red accents give the space a hint of modernity. An alfresco dining deck offers sweeping views of the surrounding foliage. It is extremely romantic in the evenings, when lit with candle light. The focus of the restaurant is French cuisine, accompanied by wines that enhance the flavour of the food. Patrons can choose from a range of superb wines from the well-stocked custom-built cellar.

Two men should be given the credit for The Mountbatten Room's roaring success— the Food & Beverage Manager Dennis Kool and the Executive Chef Nelson Chua. Both men are well known for their many years of experience and their attention to detail. Dennis Kool joined the Singapore Polo Club after 20 years in the industry as a head chef and manager. During this period, he had a hand in running some of Singapore's most successful restaurants, spending time in both kitchens and offices. His ability to direct and oversee restaurant operations made it possible for The Mountbatten Room to reinvent itself completely in less than three months.

Executive Chef Nelson Chua, whose talents were honed by the best of international and local influences, is the genius behind every beautiful plate that leaves the kitchen. His passion began at an early age, under the tutelage of his grandfather, who was a banquet chef with the renowned Raffles Hotel in the 1970s. Starting out as a teenage kitchen helper at the famed Au Jardin, Chef Chua steadily rose through the ranks of top French restaurant group Les Amis's establishments over the years. If that doesn't lend enough credibility, he also trained in the kitchen of the three-Michelin-starred Troisgros in Roanne, France.

Drop by in the late afternoons to watch a round of polo or relax in the shade with a cool drink, but be sure to stay on for the main event—a meal at The Mountbatten Room.

seats
indoor: 40 · alfresco : 40

food
French

drink
extensive wine list · Club Bar (adjacent)

features
wine cellar · alfresco dining · view of polo field

nearby
Orchard Road · shopping

contact
80 Mount Pleasant Road, Singapore 298334 ·
telephone: +65.6854 3999 ·
facsimile: +65.6256 6715 ·
email: enquiry@singaporepoloclub.org ·
website: www.singaporepoloclub.org

the villa bali garden bar + restaurant

One highlight of living in Singapore is its proximity to the rest of Southeast Asia. Diving trips to Malaysia or shopping expeditions to Bangkok are realistic weekend breaks. In the other direction, there is always Bali. Loved for its friendly people and take-it-easy lifestyle, this island retreat has long been a favourite getaway. It's a trip well worth considering, but if you are only in Singapore for a stopover or if an excursion isn't on the cards, just spend some time at Singapore's own slice of Bali at The Villa Bali Garden Bar and Restaurant.

Upon arriving at 'Little Bali', it is hard to believe that just a short walk away is a dual carriageway leading to the bustling Port of Singapore or to global giant, Ikea. The owners of Little Bali, Robin Greatbatch and Andrew Seow, have utilised their extensive knowledge of Thailand and Bali, as well as their passion for gardens and relaxing in style, to good effect. It really works—The Villa Bali Garden Restaurant is as authentic as they come. At night, lit by candles all around, patrons could almost be right in the heart of Ubud.

The Little Bali complex is spread out over a vast expanse of lush and mature exotic gardens. The Villa Bali bar is where guests can sit in an open space surrounded by friends, either to watch a little football or drink some cocktails while chatting about anything and

THIS PAGE (FROM TOP): One of several lesehans, where guests can while the night away with cool drinks and tasty bites; during the light of day, the atmosphere is vastly different.

OPPOSITE (FROM TOP): The interior of the bar is appointed in warm tones, creating intimacy and encouraging relaxation; colourful lanterns illuminate and decorate the gardens.

seats
indoor: 70 • outdoor (sheltered): 280

food
Balinese • North Indian • Thai • Western

drink
wine • cocktails • spirits • beer

features
authentic Balinese huts • alfresco dining •
arts and crafts for sale • Sunday brunch •
art gallery • Balinese dancing • private parties •
packages • weddings • seminar room •
wireless Internet access

nearby
Gillman Village • Harbourfront • VivoCity

contact
9 Lock Road, Singapore 108937 •
telephone: +65.6773 0185 •
facsimile: +65.6473 6358 •
email: info@littlebali.com •
website: www.littlebali.com

everything. There are also other more intimate spots if the occasion calls for it. The drink menu is long, with a wide selection of beers, wines, exotic cocktails and spirits. The Asian tapas menu completes the scene.

The Villa Bali Garden Restaurant is where Bali really comes to life. Authentic wooden huts with thatched roofs allow for dinner to be served in complete privacy. Romantic packages, which make full use of the setting, are very much in demand. Ensconced in a *lesehan* (Balinese hut with raised seating), your guest will surely be charmed by details such as the staff's traditional Balinese garb, premium champagne and, of course, superb food.

Contemporary Balinese, North Indian and Thai cuisine are part of the menu. Some must-tries are *rijsttafel* (an array of Indonesian and Balinese specialities), some spicy Thai salads and, for the adventurous, *pisang epe* (durian-

flavoured grilled bananas). The restaurant is also much-loved for its snack platters, which feature curries and delicacies from the spice islands.

Seventy per cent of The Villa Bali Garden Bar & Restaurant is outdoors, but for those in need of some air-conditioning, the stylish Gin Palace is outfitted with Art Deco furniture and filled with local art. The Art Gallery upstairs overlooks the lush gardens, and is reserved for special events and private lunches or dinners. It is even equipped with state-of-the-art facilities that allow guests to conduct serious business in a comfortable and relaxing environment.

The Villa Bali Garden Bar & Restaurant is constantly being improved upon and it shows no sign of stopping. The addition of the 'little food shop', Warung Frangipani, a Chinese seafood restaurant and the Bali Jimbaran (a barbeque seafood restaurant) make this little hideaway an all-round Bali experience.

tangs vivocity

THIS PAGE: Wardrobe Men provides male shoppers with trendy options in everything from clothing and shoes to accessories such as ties.

OPPOSITE (FROM TOP): Browsing through the huge range of merchandise on offer at TANGS will keep one entertained for hours; the luxurious fitting rooms allow shoppers to try on the outfit they have their eye on and survey the overall effect.

A bastion of the city-state's high street retail scene, TANGS was founded by CK Tang, who left China for Singapore in 1923 and peddled lace, embroidery and linen as a door-to-door salesman. Leaving his rickshaw behind, he opened his first store in 1932—and so began a rags-to-riches fairytale come true. TANGS' presence on the corner of Orchard and Scotts is now reinforced by a huge branch in Singapore's largest shopping mall, VivoCity. Covering all of 8,000 sq m (86,111 sq ft), it's difficult to think of anything TANGS VivoCity doesn't stock.

Occupying the entire second floor of TANGS VivoCity is TANGS Home. Here, the Asian Home section offers patrons a selection of chinoiserie-inspired lifestyle products. Aside from the traditional Asian kitchenware and tableware that are staple in most Singaporean homes, the gifts and collectibles available here, including much-loved items that would otherwise be relegated to memory, are homage to vintage Singapore.

Home furnishings of a softer type—such as bed linen, cushions and throws—and a wide variety of bathroom items are on offer in

products
high-street fashion · lingerie · homeware · beauty products · luggage

features
DHL service point · local delivery service · Atrium events · TANGS loyalty card · personal shopping

nearby
Harbourfront Centre · St James Power Station · Singapore Cruise Centre

contact
1 Harbourfront Walk
#01-187 & #02-189 VivoCity, Singapore 098585 ·
telephone: +65.6737 5500 ·
facsimile: +65.6734 4714 ·
email: customer_service@tangs.com.sg ·
website: www.tangs.com

Contemporary Home. Here, the emphasis is on chic and modern, while the Asian-inspired section is more retro and fun.

On the first floor, both men and women are treated to a bevy of desirable brands covering all styles for all ages. At PlayLab, the clothing is young and funky, produced by designers in the region or from global brands with a cultish following.

For working fashionistas seeking modern style, look no further than Wardrobe Men and Wardrobe Women. Clothes here may be slightly more formal but no less chic. Wardrobe Men, newly updated in 2008, promises a greater selection for the discerning gentleman—from exquisite accessories such as cufflinks and ties, to smart work wear and shoes.

Familiar, sought-after brands such as STUDIOTANGS, Martina Pink and Island Shop are featured in Wardrobe Women. This section offers ladies their choice of work-appropriate apparel and complementary accessories such as bags, costume jewellery and shoes.

Away from the fashion departments, the ScentBar and Beauty Hall offer a sweep of the 'superbrands' in the cosmetic business. Chanel, MAC, Origins and Bobbi Brown, among others, await. Shoppers may also wish to look out for brands such as Laneige and Darphin.

TANGS VivoCity's *pièce de résistance* is the award-winning Dressing Room, where ladies can try on designer lingerie in fitting rooms with dancing poles. A first for Singapore, the pole raised eyebrows at the launch party, when professional pole dancers showcased the department's unique selling point.

All in all, TANGS VivoCity is a store with a well thought-out lifestyle concept, where décor and ambience are key to creating an easy shopping environment.

index

index

picturecredits+acknowledgements

The publisher would like to thank the following for permission to reproduce their photographs:

Amanalang/iStockPhoto 64
Asia Images Group/Getty Images front cover (bangles), 22 (bottom left), 121 (top and bottom), 122–123
Berthold/iStockphoto 70 (top)
Blue Ginger Restaurant 128–129
Bodhi Art Gallery 146 (bottom right)
BooksActually 119 (top)
Brussels Sprouts 152–153
Café Del Mar 145 (right)
Capella Singapore 140 (bottom)
Cassis front flap (lobster entrée), back cover (bottom left), back flap (top), 142, 154–157
Chad Ehlers/Photolibrary 36
Collin Patrick 5, 146 (top)
CSLD/iStockphoto 18
DAJ/Getty Images 70 (bottom)
Darrin Haddad//Time Life Pictures/Getty Images 31 (top right)
Dorling Kindersley/Getty Images 116 (top left and bottom)
Earl & Nazima Kowall/Corbis 111 (bottom)
EggThree 146 (bottom left)
Eightfish/Getty Images 12, 25 (bottom left), 44 (bottom right)
Elangovan/Agni Kootthu 33 (top left)
enso kitchen 113 (bottom)
Entienou Photography/iStockphoto 67 (bottom)
Eric Hood/iStockphoto 13 (bottom)
Este'h Studio 147 (top)
Evnur Solid Silver 47 (bottom right)
Foodcollection/Getty Images 24 (bottom left)
Four Seasons Hotel Singapore 50–51
Frank Gaglione/Getty Images 45 (bottom left)

Garibaldi Group of Restaurants 84–85
Gavin Hellier/Getty Images 115 (top right)
Glowimages/Getty Images 19 (top)
Golden Village VivoCity Gold Class 145 (left), 150–151
Goodwood Park Hotel front cover (durian puffs), 52–53
Graham Norris/iStockphoto 108
Grand Hyatt Singapore 45 (top)
Gulfimages/Getty Images 115 (middle left), 121 (middle)
Gunther's 86–87
Guy Vanderelst/Getty Images 69
Halia back cover (bottom right), back flap (bottom), 44 (top and bottom left), 56–57
Hisham Ibrahim/Getty Images 40 (bottom)
Hsing-Wen Hsu/iStockphoto front cover (red Chinese lanterns), 102
Iggy's 43 (top right and bottom)
Image Studios/Getty Images 24 (bottom right)
Imagemore Co. Ltd./Getty Images 22 (middle left)
ImageRite/Photolibrary front cover (Esplanade–Theatres on the Bay), 2
India Se 46 (bottom), 116 (top right)
Infuzi 144 (bottom), 158–159
Ingo Jezierski/Photolibrary 68 (bottom)
InterContinental Singapore front cover (bottom right), 72 (top and bottom right), 76–77
iStockphoto 22 (middle right)
Jack Hollingsworth/Getty Images 73 (top)
Jack Wild/Getty Images 40 (top)
James Marshall/Corbis 111 (top left)

Jean Cazals/Getty Images 141
Jeffrey Coolidge/Getty Images 114 (top right)
Jim Thompson front cover (bag), back cover (cushions), 58–59, 71 (bottom left)
Jochen Tack/Photolibrary 110
Jörg Sunderman/Sentosa Cove 31 (left)
Justin Guariglia/Getty Images 25 (bottom right)
Kevin R. Morris/Corbis 28
Lisa Damayanti 29 (top right)
Lori Martin/iStockphoto 120 (top left)
Luca Tettoni/Corbis 25 (top right)
Lynn Chen 39, 41, 106 (bottom)
Mark Thompson/Getty Images back cover (Formula One circuit), 67 (top)
Matt Cardy/Getty Images 33 (bottom)
Melisa Teo 13 (top), 24 (top), 26, 27 (bottom), 144 (top)
Michael Coyne/Getty Images 20 (right), 111 (top right)
Michael Paul/Getty Images front cover (mint tea in ornate glasses), 115 (top left)
Michelangelo's 140 (top), 160–161
Mike Goldwater/Getty Images 16–17
Mumbai Se 46 (top)
My Humble House 72 (bottom left), 88–89
Neil Emmerson/Getty Images 74–75
New Majestic Hotel 112, 113 (top)
Nic Bothma/Corbis 14
Nikhil Gangavane/iStockphoto 22 (top)
Orient–Express Trains & Cruises 30, 31 (bottom right)
Original Sin 162–163
Oso Ristorante 130–131

Pasta Brava 132–133
Peach Garden Chinese Restaurants front flap (top), 90–91
Peranakan Museum back cover (Peranakan pot with lid), 27 (bottom)
Phil Weymouth/Getty Images 21, 25 (top left)
Picotin 164–165
Plush Studios/Getty Images 147 (bottom left)
Richard I'Anson/Getty Images 120 (top right)
Rick Rusing/Getty Images 71 (bottom right)
Robert Simon/iStockphoto 71 (top)
Roberto Coloma/AFP/Getty Images 15, 23 (top right and bottom), 29 (bottom), 47 (left), 105, 115 (bottom)
Sage, The Restaurant 72 (middle left)
Saint Pierre 92–93
Saraswathi Raja Krishnan 106 (top), 117, 119 (bottom), 120 (bottom)
Scott E Barbour/Getty Images 34–35
Senso Ristorante & Bar 134–135
Shanghai Tang 47 (top right)
Shaun Egan/Getty Images 118
Si Chuan Dou Hua Restaurants 94–95
Sin Kam Cheong 20 (top and bottom left), 29 (top left), 109 (top left and bottom)
Singapore Flyer back cover (top middle)
Stefen Chow/Getty Images 23 (top left), 33 (top right)
Stephen Studd/Getty Images 8–9
Steve Allen/Getty Images 19 (bottom)
Steve Raymer/Getty Images 107

Studio Paggy/Getty Images 119 (bottom left)
supperclub front cover (bottom left), 4, 96–97
Swissôtel The Stamford front flap (bottom), 73 (bottom), 78–79
Sylvester Adams/Getty Images 113 (middle)
TANGS Orchard 60–61
TANGS VivoCity 147 (bottom right), 170–171
The Fullerton Hotel Singapore 80–81
The Marmalade Pantry 45 (bottom right)
The Mountbatten Room/Singapore Polo Club 166–167
The Necessary Stage 32
The Ritz Carlton, Millenia Singapore back cover (food), 82–83
The Scarlet 114 (bottom right), 126–127
The Screening Room 1, 114 (top)
The Song of India 42, 43 (top left)
The St Regis Singapore 27 (top right), 44 (bottom right), 48–49, 54–55
The Verandah/Singapore Polo Club 143 (bottom left)
The Villa Bali Garden Bar & Restaurant 143 (top), 168–169
Timothy Auger 139
Tom Cockrem/Getty Images back cover (shophouse window), 136
Tony Oquias/iStockphoto 109 (top right)
True Blue Cuisine 98–99
Vanilla Home 62–63
W Wine Bar 124–125
Yukmin/Getty Images 143 (bottom right), 148–149
Zambuca Italian Restaurant & Bar 100–101

ORCHARD ROAD

HOTELS

Four Seasons Hotel Singapore (page 50)
190 Orchard Boulevard, Singapore 248646
telephone: +65.6734 1110
www.fourseasons.com/singapore

Goodwood Park Hotel (page 52)
22 Scotts Road, Singapore 228221
telephone: +65.6737 7411
enquiries@goodwoodparkhotel.com
www.goodwoodparkhotel.com

The St Regis Singapore (page 54)
29 Tanglin Road, Singapore 247911
telephone: +65.6506 6888
stregis.singapore@stregis.com
www.stregis.com

RESTAURANTS

Halia (page 56)
1 Cluny Road (enter via Tyersall Avenue)
Ginger Garden, Singapore Botanic Gardens,
Singapore 259569
telephone: +65.6476 6711
info@halia.com.sg
www.halia.com.sg

SHOPS

Jim Thompson (page 58)
Palais Renaissance
390 Orchard Road, #01-08 & #02-10, Singapore 238871
Takashimaya
391 Orchard Road, Ngee Ann City B1, Singapore 238873
DFS Scottswalk Level 1
25 Scotts Road, Singapore 228220
Raffles Hotel Arcade
1 Beach Road, #01-07, Singapore 189673
telephone: +65.6323 4800
siamsilk@singnet.com.sg

TANGS Orchard (page 60)
310–320 Orchard Road, Singapore 238864
telephone: +65.6737 5500
customer_service@tangs.com.sg
www.tangs.com

Vanilla Home (page 62)
390 Orchard Road, #01-07 Palais Renaissance,
Singapore 238871
telephone: +65.6838 0230
contact@vanilla-home.com
www.vanilla-home.com

CIVIC DISTRICT

HOTELS

InterContinental Singapore (page 76)
80 Middle Road, Singapore 188966
telephone: +65.6338 7600
singapore@interconti.com
www.singapore.intercontinental.com

Swissôtel The Stamford (page 78)
2 Stamford Road, Singapore 178882
telephone: +65.6338 8585
singapore-stamford@swissotel.com
www.swissotel.com/singapore-stamford

The Fullerton Hotel Singapore (page 80)
1 Fullerton Square, Singapore 049178
telephone: +65.6733 8388
info@fullertonhotel.com
www.fullertonhotel.com

The Ritz-Carlton, Millenia Singapore (page 82)
7 Raffles Avenue, Singapore 039799
telephone: +65.6337 8888
rc.slnrz.reservations@ritzcarlton.com
www.ritzcarlton.com/hotels/singapore

RESTAURANTS

Garibaldi Group of Restaurants (page 84)
Garibaldi
36 Purvis Street, #01-02, Singapore 188613
telephone: +65.6837 1468

Ricciotti Pizza, Pasta & Deli, The Riverwalk
20 Upper Circular Road, #B1-49/50 The Riverwalk,
Singapore 058416
telephone: +65.6533 9060

Ricciotti Pizza, Pasta & Deli, China Square Central
3 Pickering Street, #01-36/37 Nankin Row,
China Square Central, Singapore 048660
telephone: +65.6438 8040

DeSté
20 Upper Circular Road, #01-39/41 The Riverwalk,
Singapore 058416
telephone: +65.6536 1556
www.garibaldigroup.com.sg

Gunther's (page 86)
36 Purvis Street, #01-03, Singapore 188613
telephone: +65.6338 8955
restaurant@gunthers.com.sg
www.gunthers.com.sg

My Humble House (page 88)
8 Raffles Avenue, #02-27/29 Esplanade Mall,
Singapore 039802
telephone: +65.6423 1881
myhumblehouse@tunglok.com
www.myhumblehouse.com.sg

Peach Garden Chinese Restaurants (page 90)
Peach Garden @ Novena Gardens
273 Thomson Road, #01-06 Novena Gardens,
Singapore 307644
telephone: +65.6254 3383

Peach Garden @ Thomson Plaza
301 Upper Thomson Road, #01-88 Thomson Plaza,
Singapore 574408
telephone: +65.6451 3233

Peach Garden @ 33 in The Executives' Club
65 Chulia Street, #33-01 OCBC Centre,
Singapore 049513
telephone: +65.6535 7833

catering@peachgarden.com.sg
www.peachgarden.com.sg

Saint Pierre (page 92)
3 Magazine Road, #01-01 Central Mall,
Singapore 059570
telephone: +65.6438 0887
info@saintpierre.com.sg
www.saintpierre.com.sg

Si Chuan Dou Hua Restaurants (page 94)
Parkroyal on Beach Road
7500 Beach Road, Singapore 199591
telephone: +65.6505 5722
douhua@br.parkroyalhotels.com

UOB Plaza
80 Raffles Place, #60-01 UOB Plaza 1,
Singapore 048624
telephone: +65.6535 6006
top@sichuandouhua.com
www.sichuandouhua.com

supperclub (page 96)
331 North Bridge Road, Odeon Towers,
Singapore 188720
telephone: +65.6334 4080
singapore@supperclub.com
www.supperclub.com

True Blue Cuisine (page 98)
47/49 Armenian Street, Singapore 179937
telephone: +65.6440 0449
info@truebluecuisine.com
www.truebluecuisine.com

Zambuca Italian Restaurant + Bar (page 100)
7 Raffles Boulevard, level 3 Pan Pacific Singapore,
Singapore 039595
telephone: +65.6337 8086
manager@zambuca.com.sg
www.zambuca.com.sg

CHINATOWN + LITTLE INDIA + ARAB STREET

BARS

W Wine Bar (page 124)
11 Club Street, Singapore 069405
telephone: +65.6223 3886
gina@senso.com.sg
www.wwinebar.com

HOTELS

The Scarlet (page 126)
33 Erskine Road, Singapore 069333
telephone: +65.6511 3333
reservations@thescarlethotel.com or
enquiry@thescarlethotel.com
www.thescarlethotel.com

RESTAURANTS

Blue Ginger Restaurant (page 128)
97 Tanjong Pagar Road, Singapore 088518
telephone (restaurant): +65.6222 3928
telephone (office): +65.6224 4028
sue.teo@theblueginger.com
www.theblueginger.com

Oso Ristorante (page 130)
46 Bukit Pasoh Road, Singapore 089858
telephone: +65.6327 8378
reservations@oso.sg
www.oso.sg

Pasta Brava (page 132)
11 Craig Road, Tanjong Pagar, Singapore 089671
telephone: +65.6227 7550
info@pastabrava.com.sg
www.pastabrava.com.sg

Senso Ristorante + Bar (page 134)
21 Club Street, Singapore 069410
telephone: +65.6224 3534
senso@singnet.com.sg
www.senso.sg

AROUND THE ISLAND

CINEMAS

Golden Village Gold Class (page 150)
GV VivoCity
No 1 Harbourfront Walk, #02-30 VivoCity,
Singapore 098585
GV Grand
1 Kim Seng Promenade, #03-39/40 Great World City,
Singapore 237994
telephone: +65.6311 9162
customersvc@goldenvillage.com.sg
www.gv.com.sg

RESTAURANTS

Brussels Sprouts (page 152)
80 Mohammed Sultan Road,
#01-12 The Pier@Robertson, Singapore 239013
telephone: +65.6887 4344
info@brusselssprouts.com.sg
www.brusselssprouts.com.sg

Cassis (page 154)
7 Rochester Park, Singapore 139217
telephone: +65.6872 9366
info@capriceholdings.net
www.cassis.com.sg

Infuzi (page 158)
10 Biopolis Road, #01-01 Chromos Block,
Singapore 138670
telephone: +65.6478 9091
purdey@infuzi.com.sg
www.infuzi.com.sg

Michelangelo's (page 160)
Block 44 Jalan Merah Saga, #01-60 Chip Bee Gardens,
Singapore 278116
telephone: +65.6475 9069
reservations@michelangelos.com.sg
www.michelangelos.com.sg

Original Sin (page 162)
Block 43 Jalan Merah Saga, #01-62 Chip Bee Gardens,
Singapore 278115
telephone: +65.6475 5605
mgmt@originalsin.com.sg
www.originalsin.com.sg

Picotin (page 164)
100 Turf Club Road, Singapore 287992
telephone: +65.6877 1191
sebastien@picotin.com.sg
www.picotin.com.sg

The Mountbatten Room (page 166)
80 Mount Pleasant Road, Singapore 298334
telephone: +65.6854 3999
enquiry@singaporepoloclub.org
www.singaporepoloclub.org

The Villa Bali Garden Bar + Restaurant (page 168)
9 Lock Road, Singapore 108937
telephone: +65.6773 0185
info@littlebali.com
www.littlebali.com

directory

Emily Hill
11 Upper Wilkie Road, Singapore 228120
telephone: +65.6337 1757
admin@emilyhill.org
www.emilyhill.org

Eurasian Heritage Centre
139 Ceylon Road, Singapore 429744

Gajah Gallery
140 Hill Street, #01-08 MICA Building,
Singapore 179369
telephone: +65.6737 4202
www.gajahgallery.com

Linda Gallery
Block 15 Dempsey Road, #01-03, Singapore 249675
telephone: +65.6476 7000

Block 7 Kaki Bukit Road 1,
#02-09/010 Eunos Technolink, Singapore 415937
telephone: +65.6747 4555
lindagallery@gmail.com
www.lindagallery.com

Luxe Art Museum
6 Handy Road, #02-01 The Luxe, Singapore 229234
telephone: +65.6338 2234

M Gallery
1 Kaki Bukit Road, #03-19 Enterprise One,
Singapore 415934
telephone: +65.6841 4646
art@mgallery.com.sg
www.mgallery.com.sg

Malay Heritage Centre
85 Sultan Gate, Singapore 198501
telephone: +65.6391 0540
www.malayheritage.org.sg

MINT Museum of Toys
26 Seah Street, Singapore 188382
telephone: +65.6339 0660
info@emint.com
www.emint.com

National Museum of Singapore
93 Stamford Road, Singapore 178897
telephone: +65.6332 3659 or +65.3662 5642
nhb_nm_corpcomms@nhb.gov.sg
www.nationalmuseum.sg

Peranakan Museum
39 Armenian Street, Singapore 179941
telephone: +65.6332 7591 or +65.6332 2982 or
+65.6332 3275
www.peranakanmuseum.sg

Plastique Kinetic Worms
61 Kerbau Road, Singapore 219185
telephone: +65.6292 7783
info@pkworms.org.sg
www.pkworms.blogspot.com

Post-Museum
107 and 109 Rowell Road, Singapore 208031
telephone: +65.6396 3598 or +65.6294 0041
admin@post-museum.org
www.post-museum.org

Reflections at Bukit Chandu
31K Pepys Road, Singapore 118458
telephone: +65.6375 2510
www.s1942.org.sg

Sculpture Square
155 Middle Road, Singapore 188977
telephone: +65.633 1055
arts@sculpturesq.com.sg
www.sculpturesq.com.sg

Singapore Art Museum
71 Bras Basah Road, Singapore 189555
telephone: +65.6332 3222
www.singart.com

Studio 83
83 Kim Yam Road, #03-01, Singapore 239378

The Changi Museum
1000 Upper Changi Road North, Singapore 507707
telephone: +65.6214 2451
changi_museum@pacific.net.sg
www.changimuseum.com

NATURE

Bollywood Veggies
100 Neo Tiew Road, Singapore 719026
telephone: +65.6898 5001
bollyvegevents@gmail.com
www.bollywoodveggies.com

Bukit Timah Nature Reserve
177 Hindhede Drive, Singapore 589333
telephone: +65.6468 5736

Chek Jawa
chekjawa@sivasothi.com
chekjawa.nus.edu.sg

Cookery Magic
179 Haig Road, Singapore 438779
telephone: +65.6348 9667
info@cookerymagic.com
www.cookerymagic.com

Fort Canning Park
Fort Canning Centre, Cox Terrace, Singapore 179618
telephone: +65.6332 1302

HortPark
33 Hyderabad Road, Singapore 119578
(off Alexandra Road)
telephone: +65.6471 5601

Kent Ridge Park
Vigilante Drive, off South Buona Vista Road

MacRitchie Reservoir
Off Lornie Road

Pulau Ubin
Boat ride from Changi Jetty

Singapore Botanic Gardens
1 Cluny Road, Singapore 259569
telephone: +65.6471 7361 or +65.6471 7138
www.sbg.org.sg

Telok Blangah Hill Park
Telok Blangah Green, off Henderson Road

THE HIGH LIFE

Eastern & Oriental Express
telephone: +65.6395 0678
www.orient-express.com

il Lido
Sentosa Golf Club
27 Bukit Manis Road, Sentosa, Singapore 099892
telephone: +65.6866 1977
www.il-lido.com

Nikoi
telephone: +65.9635 1950
relax@nikoi.com

Sincere Haute Horlogerie
581 Orchard Road, #02-17/18 The Shopping Gallery at
The Hilton, Singapore 238883
telephone: +65.6738 9971
www.sincere.com.sg

Taj Air
www.tajaironline.com

Vacheron Constantin
Cortina Watch (retailer)
9 Raffles Boulevard, #01-62/65A Millenia Walk,
Singapore 039596
telephone: +65.6339 1728

176 Orchard Road, #01-19/20 Centrepoint Shopping
Centre, Singapore 238843
telephone: +65.6738 9961

290 Orchard Road, #01-13 Paragon, Singapore 238859
telephone: +65.6235 0084

250 North Bridge Road,
#01-36 Raffles City Shopping Centre, Singapore 179103
telephone: +65.6339 9185

Sincere Fine Watches (retailer)
391 Orchard Road, #01-12 Ngee Ann City,
Singapore 238872
telephone: +65.6733 0618

304 Orchard Road, #01-22 Lucky Plaza,
Singapore 238863
telephone: +65.6737 4593

www.vacheron-constantin.com

THEATRE + MUSIC

Agni Kootthu (Theatre of Fire)
Block 51 Teban Gardens Road, #11-561,
Singapore 600051
telephone: +65.9602 6437
kamasoma@pacific.net.sg

Bar None
320 Orchard Road, basement
Singapore Marriott Hotel, Singapore 238865
telephone: +65.6270 7676 (general)
www.barnoneasia.com

Drama Box
14A-14C Trengganu Street, Singapore 058468
telephone: +65.6324 5434
dramabox@pacific.net.sg
www.dramabox.org

Home Club
20 Upper Circular Road, #B1-01/06 The Riverwalk,
Singapore 058416
info@homeclub.com.sg
www.homeclub.com.sg

JAZZ@SOUTHBRIDGE
82b Boat Quay, Singapore
telephone: +65.6327 4671
www.southbridgejazz.com.sg

Prince of Wales
101 Dunlop Street, Singapore 209420
www.pow.com.sg
telephone: +65.6299 0130

Singapore Repertory Theatre
20 Merbau Road, DBS Arts Centre, Singapore 239035
telephone: +65.6221 5585
www.srt.com.sg

Teater Artistik
admin@teaterartistik.com.sg
www.teaterartistik.com.sg

Teater Ekamatra
182 Cecil Street, #01-08/10/11 Telok Ayer Performing
Arts Centre, Singapore 069547
telephone: +65 6323 6528
www.ekamatra.org.sg

TheatreWorks
72-13 Mohammed Sultan Road, Singapore 239007
telephone: +65.6737 7213
tworks@singnet.com.sg
theatreworks.org.sg

The Necessary Stage
278 Marine Parade Road, #B1-02 Marine Parade
Community Building, Singapore 449282
telephone: +65.6440 8115 (admin)
or +65.6440 9274 (artistic)
admin@necessary.org
www.necessary.org

Timbre @ The Substation
45 Armenian Street, Singapore 179936
telephone: +65.6338 8277
www.timbre.com.sg

Toy Factory
15A Smith Street, Singapore 058929
telephone: +65.6222 1526
info@toyfactory.com.sg
www.toyfactory.com.sg

W!LD RICE
3A Kerbau Road, Singapore 219142
telephone: +65.6292 2695
info@wildrice.com.sg
www.wildrice.com.sg

ORCHARD ROAD

RESTAURANTS + BARS + CAFÉS

Au Jardin
EJH Corner House, Singapore Botanic Gardens
Visitors Centre
1 Cluny Road, Singapore 259569
telephone: +65.6466 8812
aujardin@lesamis.com.sg
www.lesamis.com.sg

Ayam Bakar Ojolali
304 Orchard Road, #03-39 and #03-43 Lucky Plaza,
Singapore 238863
telephone: +65.6235 3597
www.ayambakarojolali.com

Bar None and The Living Room
320 Orchard Road, basement
Singapore Marriott Hotel, Singapore 238865
telephone: +65.6270 7676 (general)
www.barnoneasia.com

directory

Canelé Pâtisserie Chocolaterie
1 Scotts Road, #01-01A Shaw Centre, Singapore 228208
telephone: +65.6738 9020

290 Orchard Road, #B1-25 Paragon, Singapore 238859
telephone: +65.6733 8893

252 North Bridge Road, #B1-81/82 Raffles City
Shopping Centre, Singapore 179103
telephone: +65.6334 7377

11 Unity Street, #01-09 Robertson Walk,
Singapore 237995
telephone: +65.6738 8145
www.canele.com.sg

Crystal Jade Palace Restaurant
391 Orchard Road, #04-19 Ngee Ann City,
Singapore 238873
telephone: +65.6735 2388
www.crystaljade.com

Din Tai Fung
290 Orchard Road, #B1-03/06 Paragon,
Singapore 238859
telephone: +65.6836 8336

435 Orchard Road, #02-48-53 Wisma Atria,
Singapore 238877
telephone: +65.6732 1383

252 North Bridge Road,
#B1-08 Raffles City Shopping Centre, Singapore 179103
telephone: +65.6336 6369

9 Bishan Place, #01-41 Junction 8 Shopping Centre,
Singapore 579837
telephone: +65.6356 5228

4 Tampines Central 5, #02-01/31 Tampines Mall,
Singapore 529510
telephone: +65.6787 0998

Freshly Baked by Les Bijoux
57 Killiney Road, Singapore 239520
telephone: +65.6735 3298

Hediard Café-Boutique
123–125 Tanglin Road, Singapore 247921
telephone: +65.6333 6683
www.hediard.com.sg

Hua Ting Restaurant
442 Orchard Road, level 2 Orchard Hotel Singapore,
Singapore 238879
telephone: +65.6739 6666
f&b@orchardhotel.com.sg

Ice Cold Beer
9 Emerald Hill Road, Singapore 229293
telephone: +65.6735 9929
www.emerald-hill.com

Imperial Treasure Nan Bei Kitchen
391 Orchard Road, #05-12/13 Ngee Ann City,
Singapore 238873
telephone: +65.6738 1238

Jiang-Nan Chun
190 Orchard Boulevard, second floor Four Seasons
Hotel Singapore, Singapore 248646
telephone: +65.6831 7220

Kam Boat Chinese Cuisine
1 Scotts Road, #05-14 Shaw Centre, Singapore 228208
telephone: +65.6732 4675

6 Raffles Boulevard, #02-05/06 Marina Square,
Singapore 039594

Kazu Sumiyaki
5 Koek Road, #04-05 Cuppage Plaza,
Singapore 228796

Killiney Kopitiam
67 Killiney Road, Singapore 239525
telephone: +65.6734 9648 or +65.6734 3910

11 Upper East Coast Road, Singapore 455205
telephone: +65.6443 7628

1 Rochor Canal Road, #02-10 Sim Lim Square,
Singapore 188504
telephone: +65.6338 9472

8 Cheong Chin Nam Road, Singapore 599733
telephone: +65.6467 7589

11 Lorong Telok (off Circular Road), Singapore 049024
telephone: +65.6532 2889

30 Purvis Street, Singapore 188607
telephone: +65.6337 7656

1 Turf Club Avenue, Singapore Race Course,
Singapore 738078

304 Orchard Road, #01-10 Lucky Plaza,
Singapore 238863
telephone: +65.6735 7080

9 Raffles Boulevard, #01-93/94 Millenia Walk,
Singapore 039596
telephone: +65.6333 9929

6 Raffles Boulevard, #02-230A/231A Marina Square,
Singapore 039594

50 Market Street, #01-05/05A Golden Shoe Car Park,
Singapore 048940
telephone: +65.6533 6923

Changi Airport Terminal 2, Departure/Transit Lounge
North Kiosk F, Singapore 819643
telephone: +65.6542 5898

21 Amoy Street, Singapore 069856
telephone: +65.6532 6616

10 Sinaran Drive, #01-01/02 Square 2,
Singapore 307506
telephone: +65.6397 2867

298 Jalan Besar, Singapore 208959
telephone: +65.6293 8098

10 Anson Road, #01-45 International Plaza,
Singapore 079903
telephone: +65.6220 6136

1 Selegie Road, #01-03 Paradiz Centre,
Singapore 188306
telephone: +65.6338 1336

Changi Airport Terminal 1, #031-20-01
Departure/Transit Lounge East, Singapore 819642
telephone: +65.6543 4881

50 Tanah Merah Ferry Road, #01-02/25 Tanah Merah
Ferry Terminal, Singapore 498833
telephone: +65.6587 5300

3 Shenton Way, #01-01 Shenton House,
Singapore 068805
telephone: +65.6423 1161

La Strada
1 Scotts Road, #02-10 Shaw Centre, Singapore 228208
telephone: +65.6737 2622 (reservations)
or +65.6737 2555 (takeaway)
lastrada@lesamis.com.sg
www.lesamis.com.sg

mezza9 and StraitsKitchen
10 Scotts Road, Grand Hyatt Singapore,
Singapore 228211
telephone: +65.6732 1234
singapore.grand.hyatt.com

Noodle House Ken
150 Orchard Road, #01-17/18 Orchard Plaza,
Singapore 238841
telephone: +65.6235 5540

No 5 Emerald Hill Cocktail Bar
5 Emerald Hill Road, Singapore 229289
telephone: +65.6732 0818
www.emerald-hill.com

PS Café
28B Harding Road, Singapore 249549
telephone: +65.06479 3343
www.pscafe.sg

290 Orchard Road, third floor Paragon,
Singapore 238859
telephone: +65.6735 6765

390 Orchard Road, #02-09A Palais Renaissance,
Singapore 238871
telephone: +65.9834 8232

Que Pasa
7 Emerald Hill, Singapore 229291
telephone: +65.6235 6626
www.emerald-hill.com

Royal Copenhagen Tea Lounge & Restaurant
391 Orchard Road, level 2 Takashimaya Singapore
Department Store, Singapore 238873
telephone: +65.6735 6833
www.royalcopenhagen.com

Shashlik
545 Orchard Road, #06-19 Far East Shopping Centre,
Singapore 238882
telephone: +65.6732 6401

Tenshin
1 Cuscaden Road, #03-01 The Regent Singapore,
Singapore 249715
telephone: +65.6735 4588

The Canteen
1 Scotts Road, #01-01 A1/A2 Shaw Centre,
Singapore 228208
telephone: +65.6738 2276
thecanteen@lesamis.com.sg
www.lesamis.com.sg

The Drawing Room
29 Tanglin Road, lobby lounge, St Regis Singapore,
Singapore 247911
telephone: +65. 6506 6866

The Line
22 Orange Grove Road, lower lobby Tower wing,
Shangri-La Hotel, Singapore, Singapore 258350
telephone: +65.6213 4275
www.shangri-la.com

The Maramalade Pantry
390 Orchard Road, #B1-08 to 11 Palais Renaissance,
Singapore 238871
telephone: +65.6734 2700
tmp@marmaladegroup.com

16 Collyer Quay, #01-04 Hitachi Tower,
Singapore 049318
telephone: +65.6438 5015
tmp_ht@marmaladegroup.com
www.themarmaladepantry.com

The Rose Veranda
22 Orange Grove Road, mezzanine level Tower wing,
Shangri-La Hotel, Singapore, Singapore 258350
telephone: +65.6213 4486
www.shangri-la.com

The Song of India
33 Scotts Road, Singapore 228226
telephone: +65.6836 0055
services@songofindia.com.sg
www.thesongofindia.com

SHOPPING

Club21 (Four Seasons Hotel Singapore)
Club21 Gallery
telephone: +65.6887 5451
Club21 Ladies
telephone: +65.6235 0753
Club21 Men
telephone: +65.6732 4531
www.club21card.com

Déjà vu Vintage
2 Handy Road, #01-18 The Cathay, Singapore 229233
telephone: +65.6333 6630
info@dejavuvintage.com
dejavuvintage.com

Eclecticism
333 Orchard Road, #03-22/3 Meritus Mandarin
Singapore, Mandarin Gallery, Singapore 238867
telephone: +65.6735 7290

435 Orchard Road, #01-07 Wisma Atria,
Singapore 238877
telephone: +65.6732 0938
hazelchang@eclecticismonline.com
www.eclecticismonline.com

Evnur Solid Silver
163 Tanglin Road, #03-01 Tanglin Mall,
Singapore 247933
telephone: +65.6738 9053
evnur@pacific.net.sg
www.evnursolidsilver.com

Hilton Shopping Gallery
581 Orchard Road, Hilton Singapore, Singapore 238883
telephone: +65.6734 5250

Hilton Singapore
581 Orchard Road, Singapore 238883
telephone: +65.6737 2233

iSHOP by Club21
8 Grange Road, level 3 Cathay Cineleisure Orchard,
Singapore 239695

Issey Miyake
581 Orchard Road, #02-09/10 Hilton Singapore,
Hilton Shopping Gallery, Singapore 238883
telephone: +65.6732 5514

Manolo Blahnik
581 Orchard Road, Hilton Singapore,
Hilton Shopping Gallery, Singapore 238883
telephone: +65.6737 2233

Mulberry
581 Orchard Road, #01-01/02 Hilton Singapore,
Hilton Shopping Gallery, Singapore 238883

Mumbai Se
390 Orchard Road, #02-03 Palais Renaissance,
Singapore 238871
telephone: +65.6733 7188

Ngee Ann City
391 Orchard Road, Singapore 238873
telephone: +65.6733 0337
www.ngeeanncity.com.sg

On Pedder
391 Orchard Road, #02-12 P/Q Ngee Ann City,
Singapore 238873
telephone: +65.6835 1307
www.onpedder.com

Paragon
290 Orchard Road, Singapore 238859
telephone: +65.6738 5535
paragon.sg

Shanghai Tang
391 Orchard Road, #02-12-G Ngee Ann City,
Singapore 238873
telephone: +65.6737 3537

Changi Airport Terminal 3, #02-45 Departure/Transit
Lounge North, Singapore 819663
telephone: +65.6242 0777

65 Airport Boulevard, Luxury Fashion Terminal 2,
#026-91 Departure/Transit Lounge, Singapore 819141
telephone: +65.6242 0777
www.shanghaitang.com

Surrender
119 Devonshire Road, Singapore 239881
telephone: +65.6733 2130

The bagbar
290 Orchard Road, level 1 Paragon, Singapore 238859
telephone: +65.6235 5965
bagbar@thelink.com.sg
www.thelink.com.sg

The Link
333 Orchard Road, #01-01/2 Meritus Mandarin
Singapore, Mandarin Gallery, Singapore 238867
telephone: +65.6733 7185

1 Nassim Road, #02-00, Singapore 258458
telephone: +65.6733 7185
fashion@thelink.com.sg

290 Orchard Road, 01-31 Paragon, Singapore 238859
telephone: +65.6235 5965

www.thelink.com.sg

CIVIC DISTRICT

BEAUTY + SHOPPING

Actually
29A Seah Street, Singapore 188385
telephone: +65.6336 7298

Anthropology
252 North Bridge Road, #B1-77/78 Raffles City
Shopping Centre, Singapore 179103
telephone: +65.6336 3655

33 Erskine Road, #01-06/07 The Scarlet,
Singapore 069333
telephone: +65.6467 2663

Leftfoot Anthropology
16A Lorong Mambong, Holland Village,
Singapore 277677
telephone: +65.6466 3227

www.anthropology.com.sg

Browhaus
3 Temasek Boulevard, #01-004 Suntec City,
Singapore 038983
telephone: +65.6333 5875

501 Orchard Road, #03-04 Wheelock Place,
Singapore 238880
telephone: +65.6372 0070

501 Orchard Road, #05-04 Wheelock Place,
Singapore 238880
telephone: +65.6734 0070

18A Lorong Mambong, Holland Village,
Singapore 277678
telephone: +65.6467 9550

290 Orchard Road, #05-11 Paragon, Singapore 238859
telephone: +65.6737 6585

252 North Bridge Road,
#B1-19 Raffles City Shopping Centre, Singapore 179103
telephone: +65.6337 0070

20 Malacca Street, #B1-00 Malacca Centre,
Singapore 048979
telephone: +65.6438 8807
www.browhaus.com

CYC–The Custom Shop
328 North Bridge Road, #02-12 Raffles Hotel Arcade,
Singapore 188719
telephone: +65.6336 3556

9 Raffles Place, #01-21 Republic Plaza II,
Singapore 048619
telephone: +65.6538 0522
www.cyccustomshop.com

Designed in Singapore
24 Mohammed Sultan Road, Singapore 239012
telephone: +65.6733 9954
www.designedinsingapore.com

Earshot Café
1 Old Parliament Lane, Singapore 179429
enquiries@earshot.com.sg
www.earshot.com.sg

FE The Nail Lounge
252 North Bridge Road, #02-27B Raffles City
Shopping Centre, Singapore 179103
telephone: +65.6337 7595
enquiries@fethenaillounge.com
www.fethenaillounge.com

Kenko Wellness Spa
8 Raffles Avenue, #02-21 Esplanade Mall,
Singapore 039802
telephone: +65.6363 0303
esplanade@kenko.com.sg

199 South Bridge Road, Singapore 058748
telephone: +65.6223 0303
southbridge@kenko.com.sg

109 North Bridge Road, #02-06 Funan DigitaLife Mall,
Singapore 179097
telephone: +65.6333 0807
funan@kenko.com.sg

143/145 Tanglin Road, #02-01/04 Tudor Court
Shopping Gallery, Singapore 247930
telephone: +65.6836 0303
tudorct@kenko.com.sg
www.kenko.com.sg

Kokon Tozai Boutique + Café
30 Raffles Avenue, #02-05 Singapore Flyer,
Singapore 039803
telephone: +65.6337 8783
www.kokontozai.com.sg

Metropolitan Museum of Art Store
252 North Bridge Road, #01-37C Raffles City
Shopping Centre, Singapore 179103
telephone: +65.6336 1870
www.metmuseum.org

PASSAGE New York
133 Cecil Street, #01-01 Keck Seng Tower,
Singapore 069535
telephone: +65.6226 0888
contactus@passagenewyork.com
www.passagenewyork.com

Samsonite Black Label
328 North Bridge Road, #01-19 Raffles Hotel Arcade,
Singapore 188719
telephone: +65.6334 0955

Senteurs de Provence
9 Raffles Boulevard, #01-57B Millenia Walk,
Singapore 039596
telephone: +65.6334 4163
elaine@senteurs.com.sg
www.senteurs.com.sg

Sinema Old School
11B Mount Sophia, #B1-12 Old School,
Singapore 228466
telephone: +65.6336 9707
oldschool@sinema.sg
www.sinema.sg/oldschool

Sole 2 Sole
9 Raffles Boulevard, #01-47A/48 Millenia Walk,
Singapore 039596
telephone: +65.6337 1852
www.sole2sole.com.sg

Swirl
39 Stamford Road, #02-05 Stamford House,
Singapore 178885
telephone: +65.6338 5020
www.ilovetoswirl.com

Thomas Pink
168 Robinson Road, #01-09 Capital Tower,
Singapore 068912
telephone: +65.6327 9638

Takashimaya Singapore
391 Orchard Road, Ngee Ann City, Singapore 238873
telephone: +65.6738 2989

www.thomaspink.com

RESTAURANTS + BARS + CAFÉS

Attica and Attica Too
3A River Valley Road, #01-03 Clarke Quay,
Singapore 179020
telephone: +65.6333 9973
www.attica.com.sg

Bar 84
1 Nanson Road, Robertson Quay, Gallery Hotel,
Singapore 238909
telephone: +65.6849 8686
www.galleryhotel.com.sg

Bar & Billiard Room
1 Beach Road, first floor Raffles Hotel Singapore,
Singapore 189673
telephone: +65.6412 1816
dining@raffles.com

Brewerkz
30 Merchant Road, #01-05/06 Riverside Point,
Singapore 058282
telephone: +65.6438 7438

2 Stadium Walk, #01-06/07/K1 Singapore Indoor
Stadium, Singapore 397691
telephone: +65.6345 9905

903 Bukit Timah Road, Singapore 589620
telephone: +65.6464 8155

info@brewerkz.com
www.brewerkz.com

Café Iguana
30 Merchant Road, #01-03 Riverside Point,
Singapore 058282
telephone: +65.6236 1275

12 Greenwood Avenue, Singapore 289204
telephone: +65.6462 1533

info@cafeiguana.com
www.cafeiguana.com

Chef Chan's Restaurant
93 Stamford Road, #01-06 National Museum of
Singapore, Singapore 178897
telephone: +65.6333 0073
www.chefchanrestaurant.com.sg

Epicurious
60 Robertson Quay, #01-02 The Quayside,
Singapore 238252
telephone: +65.6734 7720
shop@epicurious.com.sg
www.epicurious.com.sg

Helipad
6 Eu Tong Sen Street, #05-22 The Central,
Singapore 059817
telephone: +65.6327 8118
www.helipad.com.sg

KŌ
80 Middle Road, ground floor
InterContinental Singapore, Singapore 188966
telephone: +65.6825 1064
www.singapore.intercontinental.com

Le Saint Julien
3 Fullerton Road, The Fullerton Water Boathouse,
Singapore 049215
telephone: +65.6534 5947
info@saintjulien.com.sg
www.saintjulien.com.sg

Long Bar
1 Beach Road, second floor Raffles Hotel Singapore,
Singapore 189673
telephone: +65.6412 1816
dining@raffles.com

Mag's Wine Kitchen
86 Circular Road, Singapore 049438
telephone: +65.6438 3836
mag@magswinekitchen.com
www.magswinekitchen.com

Morton's
5 Raffles Avenue, fourth floor
Mandarin Oriental Singapore, Singapore 039797
telephone: +65.6339 3740
www.mortons.com

directory

Naumi Bar
41 Seah Street, Naumi, Singapore 188396
telephone: +65.6403 6000
naumiaide@naumihotel.com
www.naumihotel.com

Olive Tree Restaurant
80 Middle Road, ground floor
InterContinental Singapore, Singapore 188966
telephone: +65.6825 1061
www.singapore.intercontinental.com

The Clinic
3C River Valley Road, #01-03 The Cannery, Clarke Quay,
Singapore 179022
telephone: +65.6887 3733
info@theclinic.sg
www.theclinic.sg

The Moomba Tuckshop
4 Battery Road, #B1-01 Bank of China Building,
Singapore 049908
telephone: +65.6536 5235
www.themoomba.com

The Rupee Room
3B River Valley Road, #01-15 The Foundry, Clarke Quay,
Singapore 179021
telephone: +65.6334 2455
marketing@harrys.com.sg
www.harrys.com.sg/Rupee.htm

Torisho Taka by Aoki
1 Nanson Road, Robertson Quay, #02-01 Gallery Hotel,
Singapore 238909
telephone: +65.6732 3343
www.galleryhotel.com.sg or www.aoki-
restaurant.com.sg

WineGarage
30 Merchant Road, #01-07 Riverside Point,
Singapore 058282
telephone: +65.6533 3188
info@winegarage.com.sg
www.winegarage.com.sg

CHINATOWN + LITTLE INDIA + ARAB STREET

SIGHTS + SOUNDS

Alsagoff Arab School
121 Jalan Sultan, Singapore 199009

Buddha Tooth Relic Temple and Museum
288 South Bridge Road, Singapore 058840
telephone: +65.6220 0220
service@btrts.org.sg
www.btrts.org.sg

Central Sikh Temple
2 Towner Road, Singapore 327804
telephone: +65.6299 3855
cst@sikhs.org.sg
www.sikhs.org.sg

Fuk Tak Chi
76 Telok Ayer Street, Singapore 048464
telephone: +65.6532 7868

Hajjah Fatimah Mosque
4001 Beach Road, Singapore 199584

Jamae Chulia Mosque
218 South Bridge Road, Singapore 058767

Kampong Kapor Methodist Church
3 Kampong Kapor Road, Singapore 208676
telephone: +65.6293 7997
mailbox@kkmc.org.sg
www.kkmc.org.sg

red dot design museum
28 Maxwell Road, red dot Traffic, Singapore 069120
telephone: +65.6327 8027
www.red-dot.de

Sri Veeramakaliamman Temple
141 Serangoon Road, Singapore 218042
telephone: +65.6295 4538 or +65.6293 4634
sriveera@starhub.net.sg
www.sriveeramakaliamman.com

The Screening Room
12 Ann Siang Road, Singapore 069692
telephone: +65.6221 1694
info@screeningroom.com.sg
www.screeningroom.com.sg

RESTAURANTS + BARS + CAFÉS

7 Sensations
16 Madras Street, Singapore 208413
telephone: +65.6298 8198

Al Tazzag Egyptian Restaurant
24 Haji Lane, Singapore 189217
telephone: +65.6295 5024

Alaturka
16 Bussorah Street, Singapore 199437
telephone: +65.6294 0304
www.alaturka.com.sg

Anjappar Authentic Chettinaad Restaurant
76–78 Race Course Road, Singapore 218575
telephone: +65.6296 5545

102 Syed Alwi Road, Singapore 207678
telephone: +65.6392 5545

sales@anjappar.com.sg
www.anjappar.com.sg

B Bakery
15 Bussorah Street, Singapore 199436
telephone: +65.6293 9010

Banana Leaf Apollo
54/55/56 Race Course Road, Singapore 218564
telephone: +65.6293 8682 or +65.6293 5054

Beaujolais Wine Bar
1 Ann Siang Hill, Singapore 069784
telephone: +65.6224 2227

Beng Hiang Restaurant
112–116 Amoy Street, Singapore 069932
telephone: +65.6221 6695 or +65.6221 6684
www.benghiang.com

Blu Jaz
11 Bali Lane, Singapore 189848
telephone: +65.6292 3800
www.blujaz.net

Blue Ribbon
42 Kandahar Street, Singapore 198896
telephone: +65.6297 7289

Bold
33 Erskine Road, G/F The Scarlet, Singapore 069333
www.thescarlethotel.com

Breeze
33 Erskine Road, 4/F The Scarlet, Singapore 069333
telephone: +65.6511 3326
www.thescarlethotel.com

Café Le Caire
39 Arab Street, Singapore 199738
telephone: +65.6292 0979
enquiry@cafelecaire.com
www.cafelecaire.com

Deli Moroccan
30 Bussorah Street, Singapore 199448
telephone: +65.9121 5121

El Sheikh Restaurant
18 Pahang Street, Singapore 198615
telephone: +65.6296 9116
info@elsheikhrestaurant.com
www.elsheikhrestaurant.com

enso kitchen (Sundays only)
14 Ann Siang Road, Singapore 069694
telephone: +65.8133 1182
admin@ensokitchen.com
www.ensokitchen.com

Food #03
Post-Museum
109 Rowell Road, Singapore 208033
telephone: +65.6396 7980
admin@food03.sg
www.food03.sg

Gayatri Restaurant
122 Race Course Road, Singapore 218583
telephone: +65.6291 1011

69 Balestier Road, Singapore Indian Association,
Singapore 329677
telephone: +65.6299 3365

info@gayatrirestaurant.com
www.gayatrirestaurant.com

Going Om
63 Haji Lane, Singapore 189256

Gorkha Grill
21 Smith Street, Chinatown, Singapore 058935
telephone: +65.6227 0806

Goto
14 Ann Siang Road, Singapore 069694
telephone: +65.6438 1553

Hillman Restaurant
135 Kitchener Road, Singapore 208518
telephone: +65.6221 5073 or +65.6296 8628

Hometown Restaurant
9 Smith Street, Singapore 058923
telephone: +65.6372 1602

Iniavan's Indian Cuisine
37 Chander Road, Singapore 219541
telephone: +65.6296 5915

42 Race Course Road, Singapore 218557
telephone: +65.6293 8705

Jade of India
172 Race Course Road, #01-01/05 Soho @ Farrer,
Singapore 218605
telephone: +65.6341 7656
www.jadeofindia.com

Khulfi Bar
15 Upper Dickson Road, Singapore 207475
telephone: +65.6294 7554

Komala Vilas Restaurant
76/78 Serangoon Road, Singapore 327981
telephone: +65.6293 6980

12/14 Buffalo Road, Singapore 209723
telephone: +65.6293 3664

komala@singnet.com.sg
www.komalavilas.com.sg

Lagnaa
6 Upper Dickson Road, Singapore 207466
telephone: +65.6296 1215

Le Carillon de L'Angelus
24 Ann Siang Road, Singapore 069704
telephone: +65.6423 0353

41 Robertson Quay, #02-03 Tyler Print Institute,
Singapore 238236
telephone: +65.6738 7429

Lee Kui (Ah Hoi) Restaurant
8/9/10 Mosque Street, Singapore 059488
telephone: +65.6222 3654

Les Bouchons
7 Ann Siang Road, Singapore 069689
telephone: +65.6423 0737

41 Robertson Quay, #01-01 Singapore Tyler
Print Institute, Singapore 238236
telephone: +65.6733 4414

Magma
2 Bukit Pasoh Road, Singapore 089816
telephone: +65.6221 0634
reservations@magmatc.com.sg
www.magmatc.com

Majestic Bar
41 Bukit Pasoh Road, Singapore 089855
telephone: +65.6534 8800
bar@newmajestichotel.com
www.majesticbar.com

Majestic Restaurant
New Majestic Hotel
31–37 Bukit Pasoh Road, Singapore 089845
telephone: +65.6511 4718

Mei Heong Yuen Dessert
65–67 Temple Street, Singapore 058610
telephone: +65.6221 1156

MoSi Café
32 Haji Lane, Singapore 189225
telephone: +65.6296 8420

Muthu's Curry
138 Race Course Road #01-01, Singapore 218591
telephone: +65.6392 1722

3 Temasek Boulevard, B1-056 Suntec City Mall,
Singapore 038983
telephone: +65.6835 7707

feedback@muthuscurry.com or
enquiries@muthuscurry.com
muthuscurry.com

Nicolas Le Restaurant
35 Keong Saik Road, Singapore 089142
telephone: +65.6224 2404
contact@restaurantnicolas.com
www.restaurantnicolas.com

Nirvana
2 Owen Road, #02-01 Fortuna Hotel, Singapore 218842
telephone: +65.6297 0400
www.nirvanacuisine.com

Northern Thai
1 Tyrwhitt Road, Singapore 207522

Pu Tien
127 Kitchener Road, Singapore 208514
telephone: +65.6295 6358
4 Tampines Central 5, #B1-K19/27 Tampines Mall,
Singapore 529510
telephone: +65.6781 2162
6 Raffles Boulevard, #02-205 Marina Square,
Singapore 039594
telephone: +65.6336 4068
1 HarbourFront Walk, #03-01B VivoCity Food Republic,
Singapore 098585
telephone: +65.6376 9358
www.putien.com

Red Star Restaurant
Block 54 Chin Swee Road, #07-23, Singapore 160054
telephone: +65.6532 5266 or +65.6532 510

Restaurant Ember
50 Keong Saik Road, G/F Hotel 1929, Singapore 089154
telephone: +65.6347 1928
restaurantember@hotel1929.com
www.hotel1929.com

Restoran Tepak Sireh
73 Sultan Gate, Singapore 198497
telephone: +65.6396 4373 or +65.6291 2873
email@tepaksireh.com
www.tepaksireh.com.sg

Rich & Good Cake Shop
24 Kandahar Street, Singapore 198887
telephone: +65.6294 3324

Sakunthala's Food Palace
66 Race Course Road, Singapore 218570
151 Dunlop Street, Singapore 209466
88 Syed Alwi Road, Singapore 207667
telephone: +65.6293 6649
enquiries@sakunthala.com.sg
www.sakunthala.com.sg

Stiff Chilli
279 Jalan Besar, Singapore 208943
telephone: +65.6297 5509
www.stiffchilli.com

Shish Mahal
#01-20 Albert Court Hotel & Mall, Singapore 189971
telephone: +65.6837 3480
enquiry@shishmahal.com.sg
www.shishmahal.com.sg

Sufi
43 Arab Street, Singapore 199742

Swaadhisht
47 Chander Road, Singapore 219546
telephone: +65.6392 0513
info@swaadhisht-singapore.com
www.swaadhisht-singapore.com

Taste Paradise
48–49 Mosque Street, Singapore 059527
telephone: +65.6226 2959
feedback@paradisegroup.com.sg
www.tasteparadise.com.sg

The Black Sheep Café
35 Mayo Street, Singapore 208316
telephone: +65.9272 1842
blacksheepcafe@gmail.com
www.theblacksheepcafe.net

Tiffin Club
16 Jiak Chuan Road, Singapore 089267
telephone: +65.6323 3189

Tong Heng Confectionery
285 South Bridge Road, Singapore 058833
telephone: +65.6223 3649

Tong Ya Coffeeshop
36 Keong Saik Road, Singapore 089143
telephone: +65.6223 5083

Zsofi Tapas Bar
68 Dunlop Street, Singapore 209396
telephone: +65.6297 5875
www.tapasbar.com.sg

SHOPPING

25 degree Celsius
25 Keong Saik Road #01-01, Singapore 089132
telephone: +65.6327 8389
ask@25degree.com
www.25degreec.com

Amba Ji International
111 Owen Road, Singapore 218918
telephone: +65.6295 2456

Asylum
22 Ann Siang Road, Singapore 069702
telephone: +65.6324 2289
info@theasylum.com.sg
www.theasylum.com.sg

Basharahil Bros
101 Arab Street, Singapore 199797
telephone: +65.6296 0432
basharahilsg@yahoo.com

Bee Cheng Hiang
189 New Bridge Road, Singapore 059422
telephone: +65.6223 7059
www.bch.com.sg

Billet Doux
45A Arab Street, Singapore 199743
(entrance via 16A Haji Lane)
telephone: +65.6294 1505
sales@billetdouxstore.com
billetdouxstore.blogspot.com

BooksActually
5 Ann Siang Road, Singapore 069688
telephone: +65.6221 1170
www.booksactually.com

Cayen
54A Club Street, Singapore 069431
telephone: +65.6227 6187
carol@cayen.com.sg
www.cayen.com.sg

Dinky Di Soviet Store
390 Victoria Street, #01-37 Golden Landmark
Shopping Complex, Singapore 188061
telephone: +65.6534 5583

Eu Yan Sang
269 South Bridge Road, Singapore 058818
telephone: +65.6223 6333
www.euyansang.com.sg

Eve
21 Club Street #02-10, Singapore 069410
telephone: +65.6573 0034
info@eve.com.sg
www.eve.com.sg

Fotografix Marketing
133 New Bridge Road, #02-13 Chinatown Point,
Singapore 059413
telephone: +65.9783 1271

Front Row
5 Ann Siang Road, Singapore 069688
telephone: +65.6224 5502 or +65.6224 5502
info@frontrowsingapore.com
www.frontrowsingapore.com

Grandfather's Collection
42 Bussorah Street, Singapore 199460
telephone: +65.6299 4530

House of Japan
55 Haji Lane, Singapore 189248
telephone: +65.6396 6657

Jamal Kazura Aromatics
21 Bussorah Street, Singapore 199439
telephone: +65.6293 3320
728 North Bridge Road, Singapore 198696
telephone: +65.6291 9419

Jap Vintage
78 Haji Lane, Singapore 189270
telephone: +65.6396 6657

Jinder's
153A Selegie Road, Singapore 188316
telephone: +65.6336 0230
jinderr@gmail.com

Know It Nothing
51 Haji Lane, Singapore 189244
telephone: +65.6392 5475
www.knowitnothing.com

Lim Chee Guan
203 New Bridge Road, Singapore 059429
telephone: +65.6227 8302
1 Park Road, #01-25 People's Park Complex,
Singapore 059108
telephone: +65.6535 0927
www.limcheeguan.com.sg

Mustafa Centre
145 Syed Alwi Road, Singapore 218108
320 Serangoon Road, Serangoon Plaza,
Singapore 218108
telephone: +65.6295 5855
www.mustafa.com.sg

Pluck
31/33 Haji Lane, Singapore 189224
telephone: +65.6396 4048
us@pluck.com.sg
pluck.com.sg

Poppy Fabric
111 Arab Street, Singapore 199807
telephone: +65.6296 6352

Salad
25/27 Haji Lane, Singapore 189218
telephone: +65.6299 5805

Sheetal
136/136A Serangoon Road, Singapore 218039
telephone: +65.6341 7125
ssheetal@singnet.com.sg
www.sheetalindia.com

Sia Huat
7, 9 and 11 Temple Street, Singapore 058559
telephone: +65.6223 1732
enquiry@siahuat.com.sg
www.siahuat.com

Silkland Trading
49 Arab Street, second floor, Singapore 199746
(entrance by 20 Haji Lane)
telephone: +65.6291 1945
prembeer@silkland.com
www.silkland.com

Soon Lee
56 Haji Lane, Singapore
telephone: +65.6297 0198
www.ishopsoonlee.blogspot.com

Strangelets
87 Amoy Street, Singapore 069906
telephone: +65.6222 1456
hello@strangelets.sg
www.strangelets.sg

STYLE:NORDIC
39 Ann Siang Road, Singapore 069716
telephone: +65.6423 9114
www.stylenordic.com

Stylemart
149 Selegie Road, Singapore 188314
telephone: +65.6338 2073 or +65.6336 3605
stylemart@pacific.net.sg
www.e-stylemart.com

Tea Chapter
9A/11 Neil Road, Singapore 088808
telephone: +65.6226 1175 or +65.6226 1917
or +65.6226 3026
inquiry@tea-chapter.com.sg
www.tea-chapter.com.sg

Venue
44–46 Club Street, Singapore 069421
telephone: +65.6323 0640

Victoria JoMo
9 Haji Lane, Singapore 189202
telephone: +65.6298 2469

White Room
37 Haji Lane, Singapore 189230
telephone: +65.6297 1280
hello@atwhiteroom.com
www.atwhiteroom.com

AROUND THE ISLAND

RESTAURANTS + BARS + CAFÉS

2am: Dessert Bar
21A Lorong Liput, Holland Village, Singapore 277733
telephone: +65.6291 9727
www.2amdessertbar.com

directory

328 Katong Laksa
216 East Coast Road, Singapore 428914
51 East Coast Road, Singapore 428770
53 East Coast Road, Singapore 428771
60 Albert Street, #01-02, Singapore 189969
101 Thomson Road, #01-K1 United Square,
Singapore 307591
Block 190 Toa Payoh Lorong 6, #01-528,
Singapore 310190

Al Hamra Lebanese & Middle Eastern Cuisine
23 Lorong Mambong, Holland Village,
Singapore 277682
telephone: +65.6464 8488
www.alhamra.com.sg

Au Petit Salut
40C Harding Road, Singapore 249548
telephone: +65.6475 1976
www.aupetitsalut.com

Baden-Baden Restaurant & Pub
42 Lorong Mambong, Holland Village,
Singapore 277696
telephone: +65.6468 5585

Barnacles Restaurant & Bar
Rasa Sentosa Resort, Singapore
101 Siloso Road, Sentosa, Singapore 098970
telephone: +65.6371 2930
www.barnacles.com.sg

Café Del Mar
Siloso Beach, Sentosa
40 Siloso Beach Walk, Singapore 098996
telephone: +65.6235 1296
www.cafedelmar.com.sg

Chin Mee Chin Confectionary
204 East Coast Road, Singapore 428903
telephone: +65.6345 0419

Cicada
7 Portsdown Road, Singapore 139298
telephone: +65.6472 2100
info@thecicada.com.sg
www.thecicada.com.sg

Culina
617 Bukit Timah Road, Singapore 269718
telephone: +65.6468 5255
shopbt@culina.com.sg
21 Orchard Boulevard, #01-23 Parkhouse,
Singapore 248645
telephone: +65.6735 8858
shop@culina.com.sg
www.culina.com.sg

Da Paolo Bistro Bar
3 Rochester Park, Singapore 139214
telephone: +65.6774 5537
www.dapaolo.com.sg

Eng Seng Restaurant
247/249 Joo Chiat Place, Singapore 427935
telephone: +65.6440 5560

Eng's Char Siew Wan Tcoon Mee
271 Onan Road, #02-19 Dunman Food Centre,
Singapore 424768

Famous 49 Katong Laksa
Hock Tong Hin Eating House
49 East Coast Road, Singapore 428768
telephone: +65.6344 5101

Fei Fei Wanton Mee
Sin Wah Coffeeshop
62/64 Joo Chiat Place, Singapore 427785

Glory Catering
139 East Coast Road, Singapore 428829
telephone: +65.6344 1749
www.glorycatering.com.sg

Guan Hoe Soon Restaurant
214 Joo Chiat Road, Singapore 427482
telephone: +65.6344 2761
sales@guanhoesoon.com
www.guanhoesoon.com

Hacienda
13A Dempsey Road, Singapore 249674
telephone: +65.6476 2922
info@hacienda.com.sg
www.hacienda.com.sg

Island Creamery
10 Jalan Serene, #01-03 Serene Centre,
Singapore 258748
telephone: +65.6468 8859

Jones the Grocer
Dempsey Hill Block 9, #01-12 Dempsey Road,
Singapore 247697
telephone: +65.6476 1512
dempseyhill@jonesthegrocer.com
www.jonesthegrocer.com

Joo Heng Restaurant
360 Joo Chiat Road, Singapore 427605
telephone: +65.6345 1503

Karma Kettle Café & Wine Bistro
26B Dempsey Hill Green, Singapore 249673
telephone: +65.6472 0221
dhi.arora@gmail.com
www.karmakettle.com

Kim Choo Kueh Chang
60 Joo Chiat Place, Singapore 427784
telephone: +65.6344 0830
www.kimchoo.com

Klee
5B Portsdown Road, #01-04 Wessex Village Square,
Singapore 139311
telephone: +65.6479 6911

La Nonna
26 Lorong Mambong, Singapore 277685
Shamrock Park, 76 Namly Place, Singapore 267226

Laurent's Café & Chocolate Bar
5B Portsdown Road, #01-02 Wessex Village Square,
Singapore 139296
telephone: +65.6475 9410
www.thechocolatefactoryonline.com

Min Jiang @ One-North
5 Rochester Park, Singapore 139216
telephone: +65.6774 0122
www.goodwoodparkhotel.com

Nogawa Restaurant
Sentosa Golf Club
27 Bukit Manis Road, Sentosa, Singapore 099892
telephone: +65.6373 7120
100 Orchard Road, #03-25 lobby
Le Meridien Singapour, Singapore 238840
telephone: +65.6732 2911
www.sushinogawa.com.sg

Oosh
22 Dempsey Road, Singapore 249679
telephone: +65.6475 0002
www.oosh.com.sg

Pietrasanta
5B Portsdown Road, #01-03 Wessex Village Square,
Singapore 139311
telephone: +65.6479 9521

Privé
2 Keppel Bay Vista, ground floor Marina at Keppel Bay,
Singapore 098382
telephone: +65.6776 0777
info@prive.com.sg
www.prive.com.sg

Provence Bakery
17A Lorong Liput, Holland Village, Singapore 277731
telephone: +65.6467 6966
www.provence.com.sg

Puteri Mas
475 Joo Chiat Road, Singapore 427682
telephone: +65.6344 8629
#01-187B Suntec City Mall, Singapore 038983
telephone: +65.6235 8768

Relish
501 Bukit Timah Road, #02-01 Cluny Court,
Singapore 259760
telephone: +65.6763 1547
www.wildrocket.com.sg/relish.htm

Riders' Café
Bukit Timah Saddle Club
51 Fairways Drive, Singapore 286965
telephone: +65.6466 9819
www.riderscafe.sg

Ristorante da Valentino
11 Jalan Bingka, Mayfair Park, Singapore 588908
telephone: +65.6462 0555

Sistina Ristorante
Block 44 Jalan Merah Saga, #01-58 Chip Bee Gardens,
Singapore 278116
telephone: +65.6476 7782

Suburbia
30 Allanbrooke Road, Singapore 099983
telephone: +65.6376 5938
info@suburbia.com.sg
www.suburbia.com.sg

Sweet Salty Spicy
392 Upper Bukit Timah Road, Singapore 678046
telephone: +65.6877 2544

The Cliff
The Sentosa Resort and Spa
2 Bukit Manis Road, Sentosa, Singapore 099891
telephone: +65.6371 1425
thecliff@thesentosa.com

The Verandah
Singapore Polo Club
80 Mount Pleasant Road, Singapore 298334
telephone: +65.6854 3999
www.singaporepoloclub.org

Turn:Styles
17C Lorong Liput, Holland Village, Singapore 277731
telephone: +65.6763 2536

Wala Wala Café and Bar
31 Lorong Mambong, Holland Village,
Singapore 277689
telephone: +65.6462 4288
www.imaginings.com.sg

Wine Network
Block 13 Dempsey Road, #01-03A, Singapore 249674
telephone: +65.6479 2280
www.winenetwork.com.sg

SHOPPING

Bodhi Art
11 Unity Street, #01-20 Robertson Walk,
Singapore 237995
telephone: +65.6235 1497
singapore@bodhiart.in
www.bodhiart.in

Bunalun
43 Jalan Merah Saga, #01-70 Chip Bee Gardens,
Singapore 278116
telephone: +65.6472 0870
chipbee@bunalun.com
Takashimaya Singapore
391 Orchard Road, #B2-01-3A Ngee Ann City,
Singapore 238873
telephone: +65.6735 2337
orchard@bunalun.com
www.bunalun.com.sg

EggThree
260 Joo Chiat Road, Singapore 427514
telephone: +65.6345 5200
33 Erskine Road, #01-10/11/12, Singapore 069333
telephone: +65.6536 6977
www.eggthree.com

Katong Antique House
208 East Coast Road, Singapore 428907
telephone: +65.6345 8544

Lim's Arts and Crafts
211 Holland Avenue, #02-01 Holland Road
Shopping Centre, Singapore 278967
telephone: +65.6467 1300

Pantry Magic
43 Jalan Merah Saga, #01-80 Chip Bee Gardens,
Singapore 278115
telephone: +65.6471 0566
sginfo@pantry-magic.com
www.pantry-magic.com/singapore

Rumah Bebe
113 East Coast Road, Singapore 428803
telephone: +65.6247 8781
contact@rumahbebe.com
www.rumahbebe.com

Shermay's Cooking School
43 Jalan Merah Saga, #03-64 Chip Bee Gardens,
Singapore 278115
telephone: +65.6479 8442
www.shermay.com

The Lawn
38 Ean Kiam Place, Singapore 429123
telephone: +65.6729 9385
www.thelawn.com.sg